Naked

Will Hathaway

www.will-hathaway.com

Creative Team Publishing
San Diego

© 2016 by Will Hathaway.

All rights reserved. No part of this book may be reproduced, stored in a retrieval system or transmitted in any form or by any means without the prior written permission of the publisher, except by a reviewer who may quote brief passages in a review to be distributed through electronic media, or printed in a newspaper, magazine or journal.

Permissions and Credits:

Scripture quotation marked NASB is taken from the New American Standard Bible, Copyright © 1960, 1962, 1963, 1968, 1971, 1972, 1973, 1975, 1977, 1995 by The Lockman Foundation.

Disclaimer:

The story in this book is fictitious. The opinions and conclusions expressed are solely those of the author and are limited to the facts, experiences, and circumstances involved. Any resemblance to past or current people, places, circumstances, or events is purely coincidental.

ISBN: 978-0-9967946-4-0

PUBLISHED BY CREATIVE TEAM PUBLISHING
www.CreativeTeamPublishing.com
San Diego
Printed in the United States of America

Endorsements

Rick Hicks
International Consultant for Operation Mobilization

I first started reading Will Hathaway's book, *Naked* out of a commitment to write an endorsement. It wasn't an obligation I was looking forward to, due to a very busy schedule and a long list of other books to read.

But, once I got into the book, or should I say, the book got into me, I was captivated by its engaging and transforming perspective of God's Word.

Due to Hathaway's creative and inspiring style of writing I was quickly challenged to reassess some of my fundamental assumptions about God's Word. His description of authenticity, shame, and love shed a whole new light on how we relate to believers and nonbelievers alike.

Endorsements

While reading *Naked* I kept thinking of friends who I wanted to give this book to. Then it hit me—these concepts are for me to deal with first, and then I'll see about sending it to my friends.

Doug Momary
Creative Director, Laguna Productions
Las Vegas, Nevada
www.lagunaproductions.net

If you want a different perspective on what it means to truly love unconditionally, truly be involved in another person's life, and truly become "Christ-like", I highly recommend this novel by Will Hathaway. Filled with insights and revelations about the current state of Christianity and what we as believers can do to bring the church back to its basic foundation, this book will make you think.

Mike Atkinson, Creator of Mikey's Funnies
www.MikeysFunnies.com

Will's engaging storytelling will draw you in with humor, surprise, and challenge—both entertaining and stretching. And his perspective as a cop and pastor informs a unique reading experience that will stay with you for quite a while.

Reverend Vernon Lintvedt, Pastor
Blessed Savior Lutheran Church, O'Fallon, Illinois

Naked, like a C.S. Lewis story, is filled with practical theology that invites reflection about the *Imago Dei* and its impact on our relationship to every person in our world. The image of God should be the uniting factor in humanity, yet we are separated by the clothing of culture, appearance, sex, intellect, talents, and disabilities.

The "take home" for me from this book was: We share the image of God from one Creator, no matter how distorted that image is due to sin's effect.

There was a resonance in my spirit with the main character in this story. Like him, I desire to strip off my shame so that God's Image may be restored as it once was in the garden at the dawn of human existence.

A thought-provoking read!

Endorsements

Dennis V. Harrison
Chief of Police (Ret.), Ft. Collins, CO

Naked challenges you to ask, "Am I really seeing what God wanted for His creation or just accepting what is on the surface?" The book will ask you to accept, love, and expose the genuine you.

Just like in police work, what is on the surface is rarely the totality of the story. This is a quick and easy read that will move us down the road to finding how a loving Father has really blessed us!

A must for us and those we love.

Naked

Will Hathaway

Table of Contents

Endorsements — 3

Dedication — 13

*****

Chapter 1
The Call That Changed It All — 15

Chapter 2
The Image of God — 23

Chapter 3
From God's Perspective — 37

Chapter 4
Less than Human — 41

Chapter 5
Naked Boy and Naked Girl — 55

Chapter 6
    Reveal, Resurrect, Restore   *61*

Chapter 7
    The Universe   *75*

Chapter 8
    Drowning Topless   *87*

Chapter 9
    True Love Never Ends Well   *101*

Chapter 10
    Carl's Church   *111*

Chapter 11
    Emma's Revelation   *125*

Chapter 12
    Till Death Do Us Part   *133*

Chapter 13
    A Surprise Visit   *145*

Chapter 14
    Wandering Souls Never Die   *151*

*****

Acknowledgements   *155*

The Author   *159*

Speaking Engagements and Products   *163*

Dedication

This book is dedicated to you, the reader. It is my hope that this work will assist you along the journey that every human eventually takes, the journey to discover one's true self.

To be fully human is to recognize that we were created in the image of God, a status we have all rejected and now clamor to regain. While most view our humanness as a limitation, "I'm only human...", *Naked* considers the possibility that our struggle is not based on the fact that we are *only* human; rather, that we are not human *enough*, and that part of Christianity's story is to resurrect, through Christ, the person within each of us that would have existed in Eden, the version of you and me that was truly crafted and molded in the image of God.

Chapter 1
The Call That Changed It All

"You're going to a nudist resort?!" I exclaimed, laughing loudly, "Have you lost your mind?!"

"I'm seventy-five, what do I care?" Carl retorted with a slight grin, holding his cigar in his teeth. "And I didn't say that I was going; I said I was thinking about going," he clarified.

"You're really taking this authenticity thing to a whole new level!" I said, wiping my eyes. I was laughing so hard they had started tearing up.

My name is Liam Haines. I met Carl several years ago, by accident really. I was working as a rookie beat cop in one of the suburbs of Phoenix, Arizona. His home had been burglarized and I was the officer dispatched to take the call.

He lived alone in a small apartment; his wife had advanced dementia and lived in a care facility. When I arrived at the residence, he greeted me out front, a slender, elderly sort, who appeared to be in pretty good shape for his age. His distinguishing characteristic was his long silver hair that stretched halfway down his back. His appearance could be summed up as a combination of tender yet rugged. The deep lines in his face told the story of someone who smiled often but had also experienced a great deal.

I greeted him with a "Good morning, sir!" as I walked up and shook his hand. He cordially replied, "Yes, it is a good morning!"

I mused that his demeanor wasn't very consistent with someone who had come home to find his place burglarized.

"Well," he smiled, "I guess it's a good thing I don't have much that's worth stealing."

He invited me through the damaged front door into his humble apartment, just a studio actually. All that was left was his bed, a dresser, a small table, some kitchen supplies, and a lifetime of photographs hanging on the walls.

"Wow! They completely cleaned you out, huh? I'm really sorry," I said as I pulled out my notepad to start documenting all of his missing property.

"What do you mean?" he asked.

"Well, I'll need to know the make, model, and approximate value of your television, stereo system, computer, and whatever else they got. If you have serial numbers, those would be quite helpful also, although most of us don't normally remember to get those off our property."

"Oh ... right. Well, here's the funny thing," he said as he looked around the room. "There's actually nothing missing. It's all here."

"What?" I asked incredulously scanning the barren room.

"Yeah, this is actually all I have. Nothing is missing. The only damage is where they kicked in the front door handle. Which I don't really understand because I never lock it anyway. I guess they didn't check first."

"I see," I said as I placed my pen back in my front pocket.

"I don't really need a report taken," Carl said. "They didn't take anything; and even if they had, I wouldn't have really cared. I just thought I should make you guys aware that someone is breaking into apartments around here. There are a lot of families and single college students and I wouldn't want someone to get hurt."

"Umm ... well, okay then. That was a little unexpected," I said. I was immediately intrigued by this guy and the matter-of-fact clarity he seemed to have on life, or at least his possessions, the few he had.

"Well, in that case, Carl, can I just get some basic info from you so I can document our contact and the fact that you don't actually want a report taken?"

"Sure," he said with a smile. "What would you like?"

I pulled out a field interview card and started filling in the boxes with Carl's information. When I got to employment, his response was "Retired."

"Well, you don't have to answer this if you don't want to, but out of personal curiosity, what exactly are you retired from?" I asked.

"Well, that's actually a complicated question," he joked as he walked over to his refrigerator and cracked open a craft beer from a local brewery.

I glanced down at my watch and noticed it was 9:30 a.m. I wasn't quick enough, though, as he caught me out of the corner of his eye and smiled, "What?" he said with a chuckle. "I told you I was retired."

"Right," I replied. "I still have 20 years before I can retire ... I guess I'm just a little jealous," I said with a laugh.

"So back to your question, I made my living doing an assortment of different jobs, but I consider myself a minister of sorts."

"Minister? Really?" My interest perked. "Well, I, too, am an ordained minister; in fact, I work as a part-time pastor at my church," I chimed up. Prior to becoming a police officer, I had studied to become a pastor.

"Is that so?" he replied. "A pastor and a cop ... that's an interesting combination."

"What church do you attend?" I asked.

Carl smirked as he made eye contact with me, looking over his bottle as he took another sip of beer. He had eyes that made you instantly self-conscious, not in a threatening way, but just an awareness way. When he looked at you, it wasn't like he was looking *at* you so much as looking *into* you, almost as if he could read your thoughts. "I don't go to church," he answered. "I strive to be church ... Besides, it's hard for a pastor who drinks beer at 9:30 a.m. to find a job," he laughed. "So what about you? You the preacher or what?"

"No. Like I said, I'm just a part-time assistant, although I do sometimes fill in on a Sunday morning if the head pastor is sick or out of town or something."

"Hmm, well, next time you're up to speak, I'd like to come hear you. I have to admit I'm somewhat fascinated by a cop/pastor," he said.

"Ha! Well, if you're serious about that, you're in luck! Our pastor is out of town this week, so I'm up this Sunday."

"Really!" he said, sounding genuinely interested. "What time are services?"

"We start at 10:00 a.m., so hopefully that's not too late for you," I quipped while grinning and glancing at his beer as it sat on the table.

He let out a heartfelt laugh, "Well, that six-pack has been in the fridge for about a month now, so I think I'll be able to hold off."

After wrapping up my contact with him, we shook hands and it was on to the next call.

I normally don't reveal so much about my personal life while on the job like that, but there was something about Carl that made it very easy to talk to him. Maybe it was his age or just his general demeanor; I'm still not sure. What I didn't know at the time was that I had just met the man who would become one of my greatest friends and mentors, and would cause me to see God, the Bible, Christianity, and life itself completely differently than I ever had before.

When hearing about the pastor side of my life, it was fairly common for people to express a desire to come hear me speak sometime, but for them to actually show up was, and still is, pretty rare. So the fact that he actually showed up that Sunday morning was somewhat of a surprise. I would soon learn that Carl was full of surprises!

Chapter 2
The Image of God

If you ever find yourself speaking at a public event and invite a stranger to attend, it's wise to notify your spouse. I learned this when Carl showed up. Since he didn't know a soul at our church, it made sense that he would sit with me, except I was speaking, therefore defaulting to my wife, Emma. Unfortunately, I was so used to people not actually showing up, I never told her about Carl. So after a slightly awkward introduction and enduring her, "I could kill you right now" glare, I proceeded to deliver my sermon, which this time was on the Garden of Eden.

After services I asked Carl if he wanted to join me for lunch, which he gladly accepted. Emma had some errands to run so it was just the two of us. As we settled around the table at the restaurant, Carl thanked me for inviting him and complimented my sermon.

"You picked one of my favorite topics in the Bible with the Garden of Eden," he said. "I know you just preached on it, but do you know what that story is really about?"

"What do you mean?" I asked somewhat suspiciously.

"The Eden story. Most Christians are so busy trying to prove it really happened that they have no idea what the story is actually about," he said in a matter-of-fact tone.

"Well, of course I know what it's about," I said, a little defensive. "It's about man's rebellion against God and how sin entered our hearts."

Carl looked at me for a moment with eyes that instantly made me second-guess what I had just said, even though I was certain it was true. He had a stare that was kind, but could make you wonder if you were right about two plus two equaling four. "Hmm, yeah, that's what I thought for a long time, too. That's what they teach us in Sunday school and seminary and whatnot, but I'm not so sure anymore."

"Oh?" I replied. "This should be interesting," I thought. If there is anything I enjoy, it's a good theological debate. "Well, go ahead," I said, eager to wow this old guy with my Biblical acumen.

"Ha! Alright, I will," he chuckled. "But only if we can still be friends afterward," he grinned. "Some people are uncomfortable being friends with heretics," he laughed.

"I promise," I answered. "No matter how wrong you are, we will still be friends," I said jokingly.

"Alright," Carl said as he pushed his empty plate back and leaned forward on his elbows, clasping his fists together in front of his mouth.

"First off, what was the temptation of Adam and Eve?" he asked.

"To know good and evil," I answered.

"Really?" he responded, shooting me that uncomfortable stare.

"Well, the text says the serpent tempted them by telling them they could be like God, knowing good and evil," I confirmed.

"Exactly!" he said. "They were told they could be like God, knowing good and evil. So if you think about it, the real temptation wasn't really about knowing good and evil so much as that knowing good and evil would make them *like God*. So the real temptation was actually to be like God. Would that be safe to say?"

"Well, okay, I can agree with that, I guess, but in my opinion the reason is a bit irrelevant; it was the action of disobeying that was the real issue."

"Ah, well, I'm afraid I couldn't disagree more," Carl stated in a gentle tone. "I think the intent is quite relevant; in fact, I think their intent is one of the most important parts of the story."

"Alright, go ahead," I answered. "I'll admit you've got me intrigued."

"Okay. Well, if their desire was to be like God, then how was that a bad thing?" he asked.

"I don't think it was a bad thing," I said. "Actually I think it was a good thing; that's why it was a trick. The serpent took their desire to be like God, which was a good thing, and used it to get them to disobey God by eating from the tree, which was a bad thing."

"I suppose you could see it that way, but weren't they already like God? After all, the story says they were made in God's image," Carl said as he took a sip from his water.

"Well … I guess they just wanted to be more like God," I said, feeling like that was the obvious scenario.

"Maybe," he mused, looking pensive, "or maybe you've been conditioned to see it that way."

"How so?" I asked, curious to see where he was going with this.

"Ever since you were a little kid in Sunday school, it was hammered into your innocent little mind to try and be more like Jesus. Right?"

"Well, yeah, isn't that kinda the goal of Christianity, to be more like Christ?" I asked.

"Yes, it is," he said, "but Christianity didn't exist at this point. So there was no teaching to be more like Christ yet. You see, because you've been taught to be more like Christ your whole life, and because you believe Christ was God, then it's a small jump to naturally assume that their desire to be like God was a good thing. Or at the very least, they were motivated by some wholesome desire."

"So you're saying their desire to be like God was a bad thing?" I asked a little baffled.

"Well, let's put it this way," he said. "If someone were to say they wanted to be like Julius Caesar, what do they mean?"

"I guess they mean they want to be rich and powerful?" I said with a chuckle.

"Right!" he exclaimed. "They don't mean they desire to be more like him as a person. They aren't talking about his character, or sense of humor, or work ethic; they are talking about his wealth. For the most part, they just want to be like him by being rich and powerful."

"Okay," I said, seeing where he was going with this.

"So when Adam and Eve were tempted to be like God, I think that's exactly where they were coming from. I think they didn't really want to be like God in a noble sense, of knowing good and evil, but simply to be gods themselves! And if knowing good and evil made that happen, then so be it," he said, pausing to allow that to sink in.

"Well," I said, as I leaned back in my chair and looked up while stroking my chin, "I suppose I might be able to agree with that, except the story was pretty clear that they would be like God 'knowing good and evil.' So it seems to me that they really were seeking the ability to differentiate between good and evil, which would have been a noble desire at its core."

"Okay, let's examine that for a second," Carl replied, as he fished around on his plate for half a French fry.

Naked

"After Adam and Eve took the fruit, what was the first thing they did?" he asked.

"They hid from God," I replied.

"No, actually that was the second thing they did," he clarified.

I took a second to think about it before it dawned on me.

"No, I'm sorry, you're right," I retracted. "It said their eyes were opened and they knew they were naked so they covered themselves in fig leaves ... then they hid from God in the bushes."

"Yes!" he said excitedly. "I'm impressed; you really know the story well," he added.

"Well, I did just preach on it, so I guess I should at least be mildly familiar with it," I laughed.

"Okay, so, theoretically, once they ate of the fruit, they would have indeed been like God in the sense that they now knew good and evil. Right?" Carl asked.

"In the sense that they knew good and evil, yes, I would agree with that, but they were not like God in the fact that they had disobeyed Him," I said, clarifying my position.

"I got ya," he said lightly. "But if they now knew good and evil, then how come the first thing they did was to cover up with fig leaves?" he asked.

I pondered this for a second and the more I thought about it, the more uncomfortable I suddenly became. I honestly had never considered this question before, and I quickly saw that a flaw in my logic had been exposed. I could tell by the way Carl was looking at me that he knew I was stumped. But his expression wasn't that of someone who was trying to win a debate, but more like someone who had given a gift and was now watching the recipient open it. There was a level of excited anticipation in his demeanor. Deciding to play along, I conceded, "I guess; I don't really know. In all honesty, it does seem like a strange reaction to learning the difference between good and evil."

"Doesn't it?" he confirmed. "I thought the same thing! If the first thing they did was to cover up after learning the difference between good and evil, then that would indicate it was evil for them to be naked. But if it was evil for them to be naked, then that would mean God made them evil because He made them naked," he again paused. "But I think we can both agree that God would have never made them evil; therefore, their reaction to cover up is completely inconsistent with learning good and evil."

I was quickly coming to the conclusion that I was now the one feeling rather exposed as Carl was bringing out aspects of this story, I was embarrassed to say, I had never thought about, even though I had been reading it since I was a child.

"Alright, but why cover up, then?" I asked, now no longer trying to win a debate, but genuinely curious for an answer to this small dilemma he had created in my mind.

"Have you ever considered the fact that man is the only creature on earth that covers its body out of shame?" Carl pointed out.

That came out of left field. "This guy has as short of an attention span as I do," I thought.

"No, I guess I haven't," I replied.

"Think about how weird that is, Liam! Every other animal on earth just goes about their merry way and thinks nothing about being naked in front of the whole world. Eat, drink, sleep, poop, pee, have sex, whatever. They don't look around to see who's watching; they just go about their lives with no concern about the fact that they are completely naked! But not us, not the human. For some weird reason we feel compelled to cover our bodies out of shame. In fact, it's actually illegal to be naked in public most places on earth. We will actually throw each other in jail for doing nothing more than being human! Think about how absurd that is on its base level!"

Again, I could honestly say I had never really thought about that before. It did seem a little weird on a purely logical level, but at the same time, the thought of everybody running around naked the same way the animals do also seemed equally as odd. Either way, his transition in thought had lost me.

"Okay, I'll agree that on an intellectual level that does seem a little strange, but what does that have to do with Adam and Eve covering themselves with fig leaves?" I asked, trying to bring him back to topic.

"It comes back to the fact that they were ashamed, Liam! They were ashamed of themselves."

"Of course they were ashamed of themselves; they had disobeyed God and sinned."

"No! Don't you see? They were ashamed of themselves *before* they even took the fruit! They were ashamed of themselves the moment the serpent told them they could be 'like God'! In that moment, they went from being perfectly content with being human to suddenly being dissatisfied with their current state, and they desired to be more. When they reached out and took ahold of that fruit, they were fully confident they were leaving their humanity behind and donning the cloak of the divine. They were certain they were becoming gods! That was the deception, Liam! Not that they would know good and evil but that they could actually become gods! The moment they took those first fateful bites, they no longer saw themselves as they really were, as humans, they saw themselves as gods, only nothing changed! Nothing changed except their perception of themselves."

I had to take a second to process all of that. Carl was normally somewhat mild-mannered but during that delivery, he conveyed an intensity that was captivating.

"Think about it," he continued. "If I told you eating this final French fry on my plate could make you fly; and if you actually believed me, what would you do?" he asked.

"Well, if I actually believed you, I'd probably eat it," I answered.

"Yeah, you probably would, and then after eating it, what would you most likely do next?"

"I would probably walk outside and try to fly," I said.

"Yes! Yes! The first thing you'd most likely do is to test out your new abilities. But what if I tricked you? What if you walked outside, told everyone around you that you were going to fly, then climbed up on this building and jumped off, fully believing you were going to fly, only to learn I had played a joke on you and you fell to the ground? Then what would you do?"

"Well," I replied, "after getting out of the hospital, I'd probably try to find a way to have your car impounded, arrest you, and seize all your assets. Although, based on what I saw, seizing your assets wouldn't amount to much," I said sarcastically.

Carl laughed loudly, "Ha! Yeah, you probably would do all those things and I'd deserve it; but in addition to that, do you think you might be a little embarrassed?"

"Well, of course I'd be embarrassed! I wouldn't want to show my face for weeks! In fact, I'd probably go into hiding or something," I said, laughing loudly.

With that, Carl didn't say a word, and without expression he directed the full force of those soul-piercing eyes right at me; and when he did, it suddenly clicked! I said I would go into hiding ... which is exactly what Adam and Eve did ... they covered their bodies with fig leaves and then they hid from God!

I sat for a moment, I'm sure with my mouth hanging open, as all of this sank in.

"Do you see it now, Liam? Adam and Eve weren't covering up and hiding because it was evil for them to be naked, they were covering up and hiding because they thought they could become gods and they were tricked. The only problem was that after they realized they were not gods, they were no longer content with being human, they still desired to be gods and, as a result, were now ashamed of their humanity."

I was taken back both by the power of this statement and the fact that Carl seemed to truly be lamenting this. I wasn't certain, but it seemed like he was actually getting a little emotional. He alleviated this curiosity when his eyes watered up and with a choked voice continued.

"We were made in the very image of God, and then we became ashamed of that image, so ashamed of it that we covered it up; and we continue to cover that image to this day. What must it have said to God for Him to have made us in His image, the crowning jewels of His magnificent creation, only for us to become ashamed of that image and cover it up? Can you even begin to imagine the kind of rejection He must have felt?"

At this, I didn't even know what to say. We just sat there for a few moments in silence before the waitress walked up and handed us our bill. I quickly snatched it from her hand, thankful actually that she was providing my mind a break. When Carl offered to pay, I promptly declined.

"Normally I'd split this with you, but today I'm not sure it's possible to repay you for what you just gave me," I said. "I'm not even sure if I agree with you or not, but you've caused me to see this entire story differently than I ever have, and I really appreciate that. I'm really going to have to ponder this a bit."

Carl smiled warmly, "Well, thank you for even taking the time to consider this. I'll be honest, I've lost most people by this point," he laughed. "Thank you for lunch, but next time it will definitely be on me."

"I really hope there is a next time, because I want to process all of this and then get together again to discuss it," I said. "Nobody has challenged me like this in years, and I'm really not sure what to do with it."

"Well, if you were challenged by this," he said, "you'll be happy to know there's a lot more!"

Chapter 3
From God's Perspective

At home that night, I knew I was going to have trouble sleeping as my conversation with Carl continued to play back through my head. I was sitting in bed holding a book I meant to be reading, but instead found myself just talking to Emma about my meeting with Carl while she was going through her nightly routine preparing for bed.

"He sounds like an interesting guy," she said while washing her face in the bathroom sink. "Where did you find him?"

I told her the odd story of responding to his house for a burglary where nothing was taken and how he told me he was a minister while drinking his morning beer.

"That guy!" she laughed and looked up while drying her face with a towel. "That guy is a minster!? Where at?"

"Well, that's the funny part," I said, trying to think back, "he never actually told me."

I gave Emma a mischievous grin as she approached the bed in her pajamas. "You know what else he said?" I asked.

"What's that?" she said suspiciously.

"He pointed out that the human being is the only creature on earth that covers its body out of shame. Every other creature just runs around naked without a care in the world," I said slyly. "Maybe we should be a little more 'natural' tonight," I whispered in her ear while resting my chin on her shoulder.

"I see," she said with a playful but tired grin. "Well, tonight I'll do just that. I'll pretend I'm sleeping out in nature; and as a result, I'd better keep covered up to protect myself from any predators. I'm sure I can count on you to keep me safe," she smirked as she shut out the light, kissed me on the cheek, and laid her head on my chest to fall asleep.

"That didn't work out quite like I had hoped," I thought to myself. As I lay awake waiting to fall asleep, my conversation with Carl kept playing back through my mind. My entire life I had always seen the temptation of Adam and Eve to have been based on a good thing, the desire to be like God. It had never occurred to me to view it from any other perspective. The idea that the temptation wasn't nearly as much a pursuit of God as it was a rejection of their humanity was completely foreign to me. What scared me most, though, wasn't so much that I agreed with him but that it made sense and there was a little part of me that always felt this story didn't make complete sense. This was so different than everything I had learned from Sunday school to seminary, and I wasn't sure what to do with it.

As my eyes grew heavy, I began to be overcome with a feeling of sadness. What would that have felt like from God's perspective? To make something in your image only to have that entity reject that image for not being good enough. I imagined a husband who had worked hard all day to put together the perfect evening for his wife, only for her to want to go out with her girlfriends, or a wife who had planned a perfect anniversary vacation with her husband, only to have him file for divorce.

From this perspective, the Genesis story was so much worse than simple disobedience; it was about total and complete rejection of God and His image.

Chapter 4
Less than Human

Over the next few days, I found myself really wanting to visit some more with Carl. The only problem was that he didn't have a phone. I remembered thinking that when I met him the first time, filling out his information card.

"You have a phone number you can be reached at?" I asked.

"Nope," he casually replied.

"Nothing? No phone number at all or do you just not want to share it?" I clarified.

"Nah, I don't bother with a phone," he said, almost scoffing. "All people do is wander around talking, texting, twerking, or whatever's the latest social media craze. Nobody pays attention to the world around them anymore!"

"Um, pretty sure it's not called 'twerking,'" I corrected him, while trying not to laugh. "So what do you do when you need to get ahold of someone?" I asked.

He laughed, "Well, that's easy. Everyone has a phone so I just ask to borrow one."

"Okay, uh ... but ... what if someone needs to get ahold of you, then?"

"I'm not that important. We went centuries without being able to get ahold of each other every second of the day. I'll survive and so will whoever is trying to reach me."

I guess he was right because I really wanted to reach him, but I was still surviving.

It would be about three months before I'd see Carl again. I was on regular patrol just driving down one of the main streets in our town when I noticed a mane of long grey hair sitting at one of the bus stops. "Was that Carl?" I thought. This guy had a bit of a beard, but I hadn't seen him in a while, either. I took a second glance and, sure enough, it was Carl!

I swung my patrol car around and pulled up just south of the bus stop as a bus was pulling up.

"Hey!" I yelled, as I suddenly blanked on Carl's name.

Apparently nobody could hear me over the engine as he picked up a large backpack and entered the line that had formed at the entrance of the bus, waiting to board after those exiting.

I started jogging toward the group and yelled again, "HEY!" as loud as I could. This time everybody heard me and three of the guys waiting to get on the bus looked at me, then looked at each other and suddenly took off running.

"That was weird," I thought. Then I remembered I was running toward them in full uniform, and had just gotten out of my patrol car. Carl saw me prior to getting on the bus, smiled and waved as he began walking towards me.

I stopped running, and his name finally returned to me as I approached, "Carl! Hey, man! How have you been?"

"Did you see those guys!?" Carl said, doubled over laughing. "You scared the crap out of them!"

"Yeah," I said, laughing to myself. "I guess they had a bit of a guilty conscience," I responded, now a little embarrassed at the small scene I had created. I looked around and everyone within a hundred yards was staring at us. Several of them must have thought I was getting ready to arrest Carl or something as they had their cell phones fixed on us recording the encounter. As soon as they saw we were just visiting as friends, they dejectedly put their phones away and continued about their business.

"Where have you been, man?" I asked.

"Chile," he replied.

"Chile!" I responded while thinking, "How does a guy who's practically homeless get to Chile?"

"Yeah, I've been down there for the last month or so. In fact, I just got back this morning. I was taking the bus home from the airport."

At that moment, a call came out from dispatch for me.

"Dang. Well, hey, I've got to go, but I'd like to get together again soon," I said.

"I would, too," he said. "What time do you get off shift today? Wanna grab some dinner?"

"That would be great!" I answered excitedly. "I should be done around 4:30 p.m. Would 5:30 work?"

"That works for me; that will let me get settled in and allow me to take a little nap."

Naked

We agreed on a location as the next bus was pulling up, and after shaking hands, I was off to the next call.

It was closer to 6:00 p.m. before I got to the restaurant, as it's rare to actually get off shift at your scheduled time. I walked in and saw Carl sitting patiently in a booth toward the back.

I slid into the seat across from him and apologized for being late.

"Sorry about that; we had an alarm call come out right as I was heading back to the station. Turned out to be false, but it slowed me up a bit."

"No worries," Carl said lightly. "You're way too preoccupied with times and schedules and stuff."

I chuckled, "Maybe so. Anyway, tell me about your trip to Chile; how'd you end up down there?"

"Oh, I have some friends down there," he said. "They run an orphanage and were planning a week-long backpacking trip in the Andes; and invited me. I built in a couple of weeks on either side of the hike to hang out with the kids at the orphanage, help out for a while."

"You don't own a phone," I reminded him. "How do these friends get ahold of you?"

"Ha, well, they don't have a phone either," he replied, "or at least a very good one. We mainly communicate via email."

"I don't remember you having a computer," I said.

"I use the computers at the library."

"I see. What exactly did you say you were retired from?" I inquired. "I don't think I ever got that from you."

"Stress," he laughed. "I'm retired from stress." He continued, "When I was younger, I did real estate and made pretty good money at it. My wife, Mary, and I got married young, but were never able to have kids. We had always planned on traveling the world when we were older but she had a stroke when she was 43. She recovered, but it launched her into early dementia and then into Alzheimer's. By the time she was 50, she had forgotten who I was and had to be placed in a care facility. I was self-employed and didn't have adequate insurance, so I had to take our savings, sell everything, and pool all the money into an annuity which I've used to pay for her care ever since." Carl's normal soul piercing stare was now blank, as he seemed to be gazing into a past memory.

"Wow. That's terrible. I don't even know what to say to that," I said dejectedly.

"Yeah, I was pretty lost there for a while," he said, "but then over time it started to become something rather beautiful. With all our money tied up in her care, it was like I had lost everything material in my life, but I still had her, or at least the person she had become. It made me realize how much I truly loved her because I knew now she could never reciprocate in any way. Even though she couldn't remember me, she still remembered her desire to travel. So that's what I started doing. I started traveling as much as I could and I'd bring back my pictures and stories of the places I'd gone. Because of her mental condition, each time she thought she had been there, too.

"Her room is covered with photographs from around the world, places she thinks she's been. So in a way, we are still traveling the world together, except I have to go out and bring the world to her. It's brought great fulfillment to my life and has given me a new purpose. She's with me in every experience I have and every photo I take, because with each one, I want to take it all in the best way I can, so I can share every detail with her."

"Are you all right?" he unexpectedly asked, looking concerned.

"Huh? Ah, yeah," I said, suddenly aware my eyes were watery. "Just a hot pepper or something in my food, that's all." I cleared my throat. "Keep going, this is interesting," I said gruffly.

"Ha, thanks. It's actually become more than just her, though. Now when I show up, everyone else in the care home gets excited; and we bring them all into the main room to hear the stories and see the pictures. So it's not only she who's getting to come along, but the rest of them as well. I've become their outlet to the outside world."

I had suspected it already, but I was now fully aware of the fact that I was in the presence of someone who was far and away a superior human being to myself, and I wanted to absorb every ounce of knowledge and wisdom he had.

Our food arrived, and we sat quietly for a few minutes, eating.

"I've been thinking a lot about our last conversation," I piped up.

"Oh, yeah?" he asked.

"I never thought about Adam and Eve rejecting their humanity; I always viewed it as just disobedience."

"Yeah, well, that's kind of the lens through which we've looked at the story for the last couple thousand years. As a result, most of us try to please God through obedience rather than through truly embracing who He made us to be."

"What do you mean?" I asked, thinking I was about to get another round of new insight.

"Most of the time, people measure their spiritual 'success' by how well they are able to follow the tenets of their faith. Christianity teaches we are all forgiven by Christ, but that doesn't stop its followers from beating themselves up for every mistake they make. They don't measure growth by how human they are, but rather by how obedient they have been. In fact, we look at being 'human' as a negative thing. People say things like, 'I'm only human' or 'It's human to err' all the time. But really, if you think about it, to be 'human' originally meant to be in the image of God. So to be 'human' was actually the highest honor; it was not a limitation, but a blessing. But like I said, we've since ruined that and instead made it a negative limitation."

Every time I talked to this guy I felt like my paradigm of Christianity was being obliterated.

"So what you're really saying is that we are in fact *not* human, that we are actually less than human because we live beneath our potential as a being created in God's image?"

Carl looked up at me with a smile like that of a proud father, "Yes! That's exactly what I'm saying; only I think you just said it better. I should write that down," he laughed.

"It kinda makes me wish we could invent a time machine so we could go back and stop them," I joked.

"Why is that?" Carl asked with a puzzled expression.

"What do you mean, 'Why'?" I asked. "If they hadn't screwed up, we might still be living in the Garden of Eden," I exclaimed.

"Hmm, see, that's part of the problem," Carl sighed. "Everybody sees this story as something that happened a long time ago in the past," he said.

"Well, didn't it?" I asked, just a little confused.

"Maybe, I suppose," he said. "But in my opinion, that's not all it is. Can you name a single person who hasn't rejected their humanity?" he asked.

I paused for a moment, not sure exactly what he meant by that question.

"I guess I'm not sure exactly what you mean," I conceded.

"It's happening right this second," he said. "Look around this restaurant right now. The most obvious clue is the fact that we are all wearing clothes, but it goes a lot deeper than that. Everyone in here has their secrets and insecurities that they hide from the world. Everyone in here has created a false persona that they present to the world in order to hide who they really are."

"Wow, you think so?" I asked. "Those are pretty big accusations."

"They aren't accusations so much as they are observations," he continued. "The cosmetic industry makes billions of dollars every year helping us to treat our physical insecurities, offering us countless alternatives to our natural physical appearance," he said. "We can change our hair color, or we can change whether it's straight or curly. We can change our eye color; or perfume the way we smell. We can make our skin lighter or darker. We have surgeries that can change our nose, our smile, the lines in our faces, our breast size, our waist size, even our very gender. And those are just some of the physical attributes!" he exclaimed.

"There are countless more emotional and personality traits that we constantly try to hide and cultivate. We often hear each other say things like, 'I wish I was funnier,' 'I wish I was more assertive,' 'I wish I was nicer, more compassionate, smarter, insightful, less outspoken, more outspoken,' the list can go on and on. When it comes down to it, most of the time we don't want people to accept us for who we are but for who we wish we were, or at the very least who we are trying to be."

As he was rattling through this list, I couldn't keep myself from taking a mental inventory of all the things that I do on a subconscious level to present myself to others.

"So it sounds like you are saying the Eden story isn't just the story of Adam and Eve?" I asked. "You're saying it's the story of each one of us?"

"Yeah, I am," he confirmed. "That's why we don't need a time machine …" he said, pausing for me to connect the dots.

"Because it's not about Adam and Eve rejecting themselves … It's about me rejecting myself," I said, my voice trailing off.

"Bingo," he said, deadpan.

"Do you remember what Jesus said about children and entering heaven?" he asked.

"You mean the part where He said we needed to have faith like a child?"

"Yeah, that's the part," he confirmed. "Except that He never said that."

"What do you mean He never said that?" I asked in disbelief. "I'm pretty certain He did!"

"Yep, and so is everyone else, but He never said it."

"I don't believe you," I said, grabbing my phone to look up the passage.

"Yeah, here it is," I said triumphantly. "Here in Matthew 18:3 it says, 'Truly I say to you, unless you are converted and become like children, you will not enter the kingdom of heaven.'" (Matthew 18:3, NASB) I blinked, re-reading it for a second, looking for the word "faith." "Wait a minute ... well hold on, it must be somewhere else," I fumbled.

"You can search the whole Bible if you want," he said, "but it's not there. Nowhere does it say 'faith like a child.'"

"I don't believe it," I said, bewilderedly. "My entire life I've always thought it said faith like a child; in fact, one of the catch phrases of Christianity is 'childlike faith.'"

"It's amazing how much conditioning can cause you to see things that aren't there, isn't it?" he said grimly. "All these people out there trying to make themselves believe in things the way children believe in Santa or the Easter Bunny, and yet that's not even what the Bible says."

"Okay, well, then if it's not talking about faith, then what is it talking about?" I asked, still somewhat dumbfounded.

"That's a great question," he chimed. "But rather than me telling you what I think, how about you ponder that on your own and let's see if we come to the same conclusion?" he said. "Besides, it's getting late, and I'd like to go see Mary before visiting hours end. I've got a lot of pictures for her."

"Yeah, sure, no problem," I agreed. "Do you need a ride?"

"Nah, that's alright, I'll walk. It's not too far from here," he said happily. "After sitting on a plane all day, it will feel good to stretch my legs. And dinner is on me this time, you got last time."

Outside, we shook hands and I started toward my car. As I was pulling away, I suddenly remembered something. Slamming on the brakes, my tires let out a little screech as I jumped out of the door and shouted over the top of the car, "Hey, Carl! One more question for ya! What's your email address?"

Chapter 5
Naked Boy and Naked Girl

"IT'S TIME FOR NAKED BOY AND NAKED GIRL!"

With that decree, I knew it was bath time. In a blur, two little bodies came bolting down the stairs into the living room and shot right past my chair as I sat reading. Into the kitchen they went, making a full lap of the house before returning to the bathroom where Mommy waited with a warm tub full of water. Any parent of small children will tell you that the workload is multiplied exponentially when more than one toddler exists in a home, but taking baths is one area where we as parents can make up for lost time. Just fill the tub with water, add some soap, and throw them all in together.

I'm not exactly sure where "Naked Boy and Naked Girl" originated, but every night at bath time my oldest son and daughter would shed their clothing, revealing their true identities, and unleash these two super heroes on whatever evils threatened our home. After making a patrol of the house, fighting whatever crime naked people fight, they would return for their evening scrubbing, assuring all was well in our small kingdom.

I walked into the bathroom to find Emma sitting on the edge of the tub and the kids nowhere to be seen, having disappeared into a cloud of soap bubbles.

As they giggled and made bubble beards and bubble hats, Emma scrubbed them clean.

"So how was your last-second dinner with Carl?" she asked.

"Ha ... mind-blowingly profound as always," I replied.

"Here's a question for you," I posed. "In the Bible, what does it say about faith and children?"

"You mean where Jesus says we need to have faith like a child?" she asked.

"Yep! That's it!" I said. I wasn't going to tell her, but I was really rooting she would also get it wrong just to feel better about myself. "Did you know that there's nothing in the Bible about having childlike faith?"

"What?! Of course there is," she said while shampooing our daughter's hair. "I'll look it up when I'm done."

"You can if you want, but I already did," I responded. "I searched the whole Bible, I even searched it on the Internet ... nowhere does it say 'childlike faith' or 'faith like a child' or anything like that. It just says we must be *like* children or *like* a child, stuff like that."

"Really?!" she said with disbelief. "I've never noticed that, I guess."

"Yeah, me neither," I said, "not until Carl pointed it out. Wanna feel awkward? Be an ordained minister and have someone point out your ignorance of one of the most basic passages in the Bible."

"Well, when stuff like that happens, you can always leave out that you're a minister and just tell people you're a cop, if that helps," she laughed. "So if it's not talking about faith, then what is it talking about?" she asked.

"I'm not sure yet, actually."

"He didn't tell you?"

"No, actually he told me to ponder it and get back to him, to see if I come to the same conclusion he did," I shared.

Emma laughed, "This guy's like some sort of a guru," she proclaimed. "Must discover answers for yourself," she mocked in an accented guru voice.

I agreed, "Yeah, he is. It's kinda frustrating. I'd rather he just give me the answers," I mused.

"So," I asked, "what does it mean to be 'like' a child?" I pondered while watching my kids bury their faces in the water to blow bubbles, causing them both to laugh and splash hysterically every time they came up for air.

Bedtime was always one of my favorite routines when the kids were little. I loved getting them into their pajamas and tucking them into bed. I never got enough of their little expressions as we did story time each night, or the innocence of their little prayers. The images of them in my mind with their eyes closed tight and their little bodies still too small for their heads make me smile to this day.

After planting a kiss on each of their foreheads and wishing them goodnight, I returned to our room to give Emma a little break from the baby. As I held him in my arms, rocking him to sleep back and forth, I imagined Jesus laughing and playing with the small children of Galilee after admonishing His disciples for trying to keep them from Him.

I also thought of my conversations with Carl and the concept of people rejecting themselves. "It's funny," I thought, "every night we are able to throw our kids in the bathtub completely naked and they hardly seem to notice or even care really. It's like there's no inhibition, no concern, no ... *shame!*"

"That's it! There's no shame!" I said out loud, causing the baby to stir.

"Shh!" Emma said in a hushed tone. "You're going to wake the baby."

"Sorry," I whispered, gently laying him in his crib. "I've got to email Carl."

"Email?" Emma asked in a baffled tone. "Why don't you just call him?"

Chapter 6
Reveal, Resurrect, Restore

"Uganda! What the heck is he doing in Uganda?" I exclaimed.

"Who's in Uganda?" Emma inquired, sipping her morning tea.

"I just got an email from Carl. That's why I haven't heard from him in so long. Apparently he's been over there the last few weeks helping to dig wells for some sort of children's organization that takes in child refugees," I replied. "He says he'll be back in about two weeks."

"Of course, he is," Emma said laughing. "That guy is amazing."

"I don't know how he affords it," I questioned. "From what I understand, all his money goes into his wife's care.

Maybe he's like one of those millionaire hermits who live like they are poor?" I said in jest.

"Well, with all of his travels around the world, he's not doing a very good job of being a hermit," Emma chimed.

As I was quickly learning with Carl, time is a very relative thing. After saying he'd be back in two weeks, I got an email from him three and a half weeks later, saying he had just arrived home.

We arranged to get together that weekend to hike Camelback Mountain, a popular landmark in the Phoenix area.

There is something fragrant about the smell of the Sonoran Desert in the early morning, especially after a rain. I picked Carl up at his apartment, and we arrived at the trailhead just before dawn to get started up the mountain prior to the heat of day. The ground was damp but not muddy, thanks to the rare showers that had come through the night before. The sweet aroma of desert sage filled the air as hummingbirds buzzed back and forth between the cactus flowers.

"So, Uganda, eh?" I said as we began trudging up the well-worn trail created by hundreds of people who hike this mountain every year.

"Huh? Oh, yeah, yeah, I have a friend over there who works with refugee children, and they were digging wells," he replied.

"How do you find all of these friends around the world?" I asked.

Carl laughed while stepping over a large rock, "Well, it's amazing all the connections you can make when you put your cell phone down and actually talk to the people around you," he jokingly jabbed.

"Yeah, I guess," I replied. "I'll have to get better at that."

"So not that it's any of my business, and you don't have to answer this if you don't want to, but based on your story about all of your funds going to care for Mary, how can you possibly afford all of these exotic trips?" I asked.

"You gotta know how to go on the cheap!" he said with a chuckle. "First off, I work odd jobs as a handy man, substitute teacher, mechanic, whatever, to make a little extra cash here and there. That, combined with my and Mary's social security, pretty well takes care of the basic bills; and as you saw, I don't have a lot of expenses," he said. "As far as the travel, I mostly stay with friends I've made along the way, so that doesn't cost much."

"What about the flights?" I asked. "Those can't be cheap."

"Ah, yes! That's the best deal of all," he said excitedly. "One of the older ladies at Mary's home has a son who is an airline pilot. We've become friends through the care home, and he decided to add me on as a travel companion, so I get all the same deals he gets, which costs next to nothing. The main thing is I've got to be willing to fly standby, which is easy for me since I'm almost always traveling solo."

"Wow, that's pretty cool!"

"Yeah, he's been divorced for a number of years now and told me he'll keep me on his account until he finds a new woman. I have mixed feelings because I don't want the guy to be lonely, but I also don't want to lose my cheap flights," he laughed. "I figure it's only a matter of time, so I'm trying to travel as much as I can, although it's been a couple years now, so who knows."

As we continued up the trail, we passed a man and his daughter sitting on a rock. She was a cute kid about ten years old or so, with her water bottle and baseball cap, resting her little legs. Her expression was one of dissatisfaction; and as we passed, she looked up at me and shared, "This sucks!"

I tried to contain my laughter as I looked at her father, who looked back at me with a helpless shrug of his shoulders.

"It might suck now, but the view at the top is worth it!" I said, trying to encourage her. I couldn't help but smile to myself at the innocent honesty found only in children.

"So I've noticed there seems to be a common theme between your trips and working with children, the refugee camp, the orphanage, and whatnot."

"Yeah, there is," he answered. "That's not accidental. A couple years ago I came back from one of my trips, and the staff at Mary's assisted living facility told me she had been staring at all of the pictures I had brought of children. Apparently, it didn't matter what they looked like, she thought they were all hers. She would point out different ones and not be able to give their names but would have some sort of a story about their lives; of course, it would change every time, but each time she would light up with the same pride as any real mom would while talking about her kids. Finally, I just went with it.

"We were never able to have kids of our own, so she never got to be a mom. If I couldn't give her kids the natural way, I finally decided I'd give her all the children I could this way, so all of my trips started to focus around helping kids. Every time I come back, she has more pictures of kids to love and create stories about."

"So is that hard for you? I mean, knowing none of it is real and all?" I immediately regretted my choice of words with that question or even asking it. It was basically one of those things that thoughtlessly gets blurted out while trying to fill silence.

"No, not really," he continued, unaffected by the insensitive nature of what I said. "It's real for her, so that's real enough for me."

I decided to change the subject to a less sensitive topic before something else stupid came out of my mouth.

"I think I've come to a conclusion regarding our last conversation about becoming like a child," I offered.

"Oh, yeah," he recollected. "That was a while ago! Wow, how time flies! Okay, so what did you conclude?" he asked.

"Well, I think it is talking about how kids are authentic and real," I said.

"Good!" Carl exclaimed. "That makes me feel better because that's the direction I've taken with it, too. So elaborate: what makes you think that?" he asked.

Naked

I pondered a second, gathering my thoughts. "In a way, Adam and Eve were just like little kids in the garden because they ran around naked and thought nothing of it, the same way my little ones think nothing of it when they are running around naked. They aren't ashamed of their bodies."

"Agreed," Carl stated. He continued, "And I'll even take that a step farther: they aren't ashamed of themselves, either. They feel what they feel, they think what they think, and they don't hide it. They are perfectly content being naked not only physically, but emotionally and spiritually as well."

"I was thinking about it on my way into work the other day," I said, pausing a moment to take in the view of the city during our ascent. "There are aspects of the story that apply to everyone. We all start out naked and unashamed, the same way Adam and Eve did; and then as we get older, we start to learn things, or maybe better said is that we are taught things. We run around naked until someone teaches us we are too old for that, we speak our mind until someone teaches us that's not polite, etc. We don't take from a Tree of Knowledge, but we do obtain knowledge. We are taught 'good and evil,' and one of the things everybody learns is to eventually cover up both their body and their hearts."

"Isn't that interesting?" Carl mused. "What's really intriguing is when you take that Eden story and then compare it to Christ."

"How's that?" I asked.

"Well, we already talked about how He said that to inherit the kingdom we must become like children, but beyond that, the only time you really saw Him flip out was when it came to hypocrisy."

"Okay," I said, trying to think of some examples.

"Think about it: when did you ever see Jesus rip someone for being a thief or an adulterer or a drunk or anything like that?" he asked.

"Well, I mean, I guess he told the adulterous woman to 'go and sin no more,'" I said. "That's about all I can think of at the moment."

"Yeah, He did," Carl agreed, "but that's quite a bit different than the way He blew up on the Pharisees when He called them a den of vipers and whitewashed tombs and whatnot. You don't see Him going into the house of the adulteress and flipping over tables and trashing her place the way He did in the Temple."

"No, I guess you're right about that," I agreed. "So it's almost like Jesus saw hypocrisy as the worst sin of all when you look at it from that perspective."

"Didn't He tell the religious leaders that thieves and prostitutes and sinners were entering the kingdom of heaven ahead of them?" Carl asked. "All those people may have been dysfunctional and broken, but they were at least real about it."

"That's actually pretty profound," I observed. "One of the things I've noticed in law enforcement is how much more transparent a lot of these people we call 'criminals' tend to be, compared to the rest of us. I mean, yeah, you have your con men and all that, but I've always been amazed at how many of them will just willingly open up about things in their lives that the rest of us would never reveal. Many of them will tell you about their drug addiction or sex addiction or whatever their issue might be. It's sad, really, because they aren't very judgmental either. That's sometimes why it's so hard for them to get out of their messed up lives; they know they are messed up but at least they aren't judged by the messed up people around them."

"Yeah, that is sad," Carl said. "Then when they come to church, they feel judged; so they retreat back to their broken but safe world," he sighed. "A lot of times it's easier to be broken than it is to be judged."

As I pondered what Carl had just said, I felt myself feeling a wave of compassion for the anguish these people must feel when they come to the church seeking acceptance but instead being met with more rejection.

"So would it be safe to guess that the reason Jesus loved hanging out with these people, was because they were real?" I asked.

"Well, not being Christ, that's hard to say," Carl said, "but look at it this way. Jesus was, in my opinion, the most authentic guy who ever lived. If we look at being good as the most pleasing thing to Christ, then the religious leaders should have been His favorites. Because, even though they were fake, they did all the things they were supposed to do. But if being real was what was most important to Him, then that makes sense as to why He loved the down and out. They might not have been choir members, but they were at least real. In fact, since Jesus was so authentic, maybe He had to go to the sinners to find people that were most like Him." Carl paused for a moment as we summited the mountain moments before the sun crested the horizon.

"Wow!" I mumbled. "What a role reversal that would be. We've always been taught that to be most like Christ we should be 'good.' You know, don't drink, cuss, smoke, whatever. What if being like Jesus is way more about being real than being good? That changes everything about His interactions with the sinners. In that case they would have actually been way ahead of the religious."

"Yep," Carl agreed. "Speaking of smoking ... cigar?" I turned around to find Carl holding one cigar in his mouth and extending a second one out to me.

"I think I will," I said with a laugh. "Thank you."

This was a rare morning, in that nobody else was on the mountain. We both sat in pensive silence and smoked our cigars, the city below coming to life as the rising sun caused the mountain shadows to recede along the valley floor.

"So kids and sinners might be more like Christ in that they are authentic," I said, breaking the silence, "but kids can be little brats, too," I laughed.

"Ha! Yes, they can," he confirmed, "but kids are *authentic* little brats. And yes, sinners can be pretty destructive, but that's why it doesn't just end with authenticity. There is one more factor that has to exist for it all to come together.

"Oh, yeah?" I asked, blowing out a plume of smoke. "What's that?"

Carl smiled and replied with his cigar in his teeth, "Love."

"Love, eh?" I retorted as we started our journey back down the mountain. "Alright, go ahead."

"Well, having no actual children of my own, I can't exactly speak from personal experience here, but as an outsider looking in, this is what seems to make sense to me," Carl began.

"They say that there is no love like the love a parent has for a child. As a parent yourself, would you agree with that?" Carl asked.

"Undoubtedly!" I exclaimed. "There is nothing like it that I've ever experienced; it's the most pure and tender love of all… I can't really even explain it."

"Not to be too cerebral about it, but I find it interesting that the deepest love that can be found in life takes place in the most authentic possible environment," he continued. "There is probably no one on earth a person will ever know better than their child, especially in the very early stages of life. When they are little, you might even know them better than they know themselves. You change their diapers, you feed them, you teach them, you make them laugh, you see their tantrums, you see their personalities develop; while they are little, nothing is held back from you. They tell you when they are hungry or angry or sad, they tell you everything, and you have access to every part of their lives, everything! And in that environment of fully and completely knowing someone, a type of love is born that can't be found anywhere else."

"Hmm, I guess I've never really looked at it that way, but that does kinda make sense," I replied.

"In every other relationship in life, we all hold something back, we all have that little nagging fear that if the people who loved us really knew us, they wouldn't love us anymore. As a result, we keep our deepest, darkest secrets to ourselves and, in turn, never really learn who truly loves us and who doesn't because nobody is ever allowed to completely know us. We don't want to be completely and totally known by others; that idea is terrifying to us."

"But not to a little kid," I said softly, half to myself and half to Carl as the concept started to become clear. "A little kid doesn't know not to be himself and hasn't lived long enough to know to feel ashamed of something, and therefore hides nothing ... interesting."

"Yes, but as the children grow, they will learn to hide their own secrets, many out of fear of disappointing their parents or losing their love, which will eventually change the dynamics of the relationship," Carl added. "That's why I think Jesus was so adamant about people being authentic. If love was His deepest calling to us, then He would have had to also call us to authenticity, because without authenticity, true love can't exist. It would just be an illusion."

"An illusion because if none of us are completely real with each other, then that means we don't really love each other, we just love the person we present to each other," I summarized. "Wow ..." I said, my voice trailing off.

"So in a sense," I continued, "it's almost like Jesus was calling us back to the Garden of Eden, to go back to being 'naked' in the sense that we were authentic, so we can experience the love God always meant for us to have!"

"That's my take on it, anyway," Carl confirmed. "When we stop being authentic, it's like the person we were meant to be dies, in that we stop being that person. I think God wants to restore us to the person we were always meant to be, so, in a sense, to 'resurrect' that person. But the scary part for us is, that would mean the path to true love requires us to be willing to reveal who we really are," Carl said.

"Hmm, that does feel risky," I agreed. "To be fully revealed ... you're right, that does sound terrifying. So in a nutshell, you're saying God wants us to be willing to reveal who we really are, so He can resurrect the person we've all put to death, so He can restore us to the person we were always meant to be?"

"I'm not sure I could have said that better myself," Carl gleamed like a proud father. "Reveal. Resurrect. Restore. That's a great summarization, Liam! Someone should write that down."

Chapter 7
The Universe

Being that police officers aren't paramedics, having to do CPR is something we are trained on, but not something we do on a regular basis. For us, doing CPR on anyone is a little out of our comfort zone. Having to do it on an infant is way out of our comfort zone.

I was the first officer on scene to a sudden infant death call and immediately began compressions on the little guy as soon as I arrived. As I fervently worked to try to revive him, I was familiar enough with mortality to know he was already gone and had been for a while, but when it's a baby, you try anyway. I'm still somewhat haunted by the feeling of his cold little lifeless lips on mine as I tried to breathe air into his tiny lungs. The sound of the fire engine was like an orchestra of hope in the midst of the wails of his young mother, lamenting her tragic loss. I turned compressions over to the paramedics but would soon have my fears confirmed; it was too late.

Emma can always tell when I've had a rough day at work; she knows me so well that I can't hide it, nor do I even try anymore. It took me awhile to learn it was actually a lot healthier for me to share these things with her rather than try to "protect" her from some of the more troubling aspects of my job.

After visiting and decompressing for a bit, I went outside and played with the kids before dinner. I spent a little extra time tucking each of them in that night, especially grateful for the blessing each of them is in my life.

When I returned to the bedroom to shower and change, I noticed a new email had popped up on my phone. It was from Carl:

> "Hey Liam,
> After our hike last week I was wondering if you wanted to join me in a couple weeks to hike the Grand Canyon. I'm going to Havasupai Falls.
> Just let me know.
> Carl"

Havasupai Falls happens to be one of my favorite places on earth.

Naked

"I think you should go," Emma said. "It's been a while since you've been backpacking and I think that after today the break would be good for you."

Never needing much of an excuse to go backpacking, and having not taken a day off in quite some time, I agreed and responded to Carl, letting him know that I was on board. I immediately began looking forward to having some time to let off some steam.

I've made the 13-mile trek down to the falls three times in my life, and each time it seemed more spectacular than the last. It's truly one of the most beautiful places in the world. If you've never been there, the trailhead is located along the south rim of the Grand Canyon, several hours northwest of Flagstaff, Arizona.

We reached the trailhead at dusk and hiked down the switchbacks to the canyon floor. At the base of the giant walls, we pulled off the trail and camped for the night. This part of the canyon is extremely dry and desolate, with the cool blue-green waters of Havasu Canyon still several miles away. The area is so full of scrub brush and rocks that it's difficult to find a place to set up a tent. After surveying the area, Carl and I located a rock ledge at the edge of a sandy wash that was relatively flat and decided to spend this particular evening out under the stars. As we laid in our sleeping bags on that cloudless night, the universe put itself on display. Being so far from any city lights, the heavens came alive as each star seemed to be trying to outshine all the rest. We could see the Milky Way stretched across the sky like the wake from a giant ship. Jupiter beamed brightly overhead, and the constellations followed their ancient paths, dancing through the night in a performance seen by an untold number of eyes through the centuries. Now it was our turn to take in these marvelous sights that had been wowing mankind since our inception.

The night sky always had a way of making me feel quite insignificant, but during this particular experience, the sense of smallness was magnified by the towering canyon walls that framed this beautiful scene. I remember being taken with how silent it was, as this area is so dry and empty that there are not even crickets to chirp. It was as if nature itself was remaining reverently silent in the presence of heaven's cathedral.

"You think there's other life out there, Carl?" I finally asked, peering out into the universe.

"I don't know," Carl replied. "Part of me kind of hopes so."

"Why is that?" I asked.

"Well, if you think about it, if we are the only life in the universe, then there are hundreds of millions of stars and planets way outside of our view that are just floating out there in space with nobody to admire them," he said.

As usual, leave it to Carl to provide perspectives that have never occurred to me.

"This place is magnificent," he continued. "Imagine how sad it would be if mankind didn't exist? Imagine how sad it would be for this incredibly beautiful and marvelous creation to exist and there not be a creature within it that had the capacity to peer into the heavens in awe, to smile at the rumble of thunder, or appreciate the majestic beauty of a waterfall. Sure, other creatures can see and hear these things, but do they truly appreciate the magnitude of it all the way we can?

"If we are the only intelligent life in the universe, then we have such a huge responsibility, for it is only through us that the universe can truly come alive. How tragic would it be for the heavens to have no one to see them? And for the roar of the ocean waves to have no one to hear them? What if the flower had no one to take in its fragrant aromas? In a way, the universe would cease to have meaning without a conscience being within it to appreciate it. Without man, it would simply be a galactic machine that would continue ticking on in silent obscurity because we are the ones who give it audience," he paused. "So, yes, yes, I hope there is other life out there to share this great responsibility with us because sometimes I worry about man's capacity to fully appreciate it."

I found myself briefly distracted from the sky and now looking incredulously over at Carl, and he was entranced upward.

"Where the heck do you come up with this stuff?" I asked emphatically.

Carl laughed, "Well, when you spend a lot of time by yourself, you find your mind tends to wander a bit."

"That is a good point, though," a new thought dawning on me. "The universe is so big that even if there is other life out there, it's still likely that there are large portions of it that nobody will ever see or experience. And that's especially true if we are in fact the only planet with intelligent life. So based on what you just said, there are probably incredibly wonderful and beautiful things out there right this second that nobody aside from God will ever even know about."

"Yeah, you're probably right," Carl sighed. "Pretty sad, isn't it?"

"Very sad," I confirmed. "It kinda makes you wonder why He made such an enormous universe if the vast majority of it will never be appreciated. Seems like a real waste."

Naked

"Maybe," Carl's voice perked. "Or maybe it was always part of the plan."

"How so?" I asked.

"Well, suppose mankind really was created in God's image," he said. "If that's the case, then what kind of potential would a creature made in God's image have?"

"I suppose a lot," I reasoned.

"Yeah, a whole lot, I'd say. If God is limitless, then it would make sense to me that a creature created in His image would have almost limitless potential, wouldn't it?"

"Hmm, well, yeah, I guess it would," I said, starting to see where he might be headed.

"Do you remember what God's first command was to Adam and Eve in the Garden?" Carl asked.

"Don't eat the fruit?" I asked

"Nope!" he said gleefully. "The first command was to be fruitful and multiply!" he laughed. "That's how we know God is male," he quipped.

"Ha! I'll have to remember that when I get home!" I mimicked a conversation with my wife sounding as sincere as I could: "Now listen, dear, and remember this is a command from God, and we wouldn't want to disobey the Lord!"

"Ha, ha! Well, I'm sure that tactic will work well," Carl laughed. "But in all seriousness, let's just assume man had never sinned and actually fulfilled that first command of God. If that had occurred, it would have only been a matter of time before we really did fill the Earth."

"Heck, we might fill it anyway the way the population keeps growing," I interrupted.

"Yeah, we might," he said. "So then what? What do we do then?" Carl asked.

"So are you saying you think it's been God's plan for us to go into space all along?" I asked.

"I'd like to think so." Carl explained, "I mean, I have a hard time believing we caught Him by surprise when we were able to get into orbit. Mankind has always possessed the ability to have all the technologies we have today. The resources were always there, but we were too busy killing, raping, and pillaging each other throughout history to discover these things. And most of the technologies we have come up with were developed for or during war, again, with the intent of killing each other. Even in our broken state we were able to get a rickety little space craft from here to the moon. Sure, it took us several thousand years, but we did it. How many other amazing technologies exist out there that we just haven't discovered yet?"

"That's interesting," I interjected, pondering Carl's words. I continued, "And on the other side of that, we also seem hell bent on holding each other back as well. How many times does someone come up with a new innovation that threatens to revolutionize an industry, only to be put out of business by those who currently own the majority of the market? Seems like that happens all the time," I lamented.

"It does," Carl nodded. "If I invent something and get rich off of it and you invent something better, that's going to take my business away, then I go after you. But what if God's original plan for us had actually played out? What if we lived in a world where we didn't try and blow each other up over land or resources? What if we lived in a world where we did not feel threatened by each other's successes and in turn never held each other back? What if we lived in a world where there was no genocide, where we didn't let people starve, where we actually loved and encouraged each other? What could be accomplished then? Imagine what we could cure, what we could discover, what we could become if we, as an entire species, actually tried to bring out the absolute best in each other rather than tearing one another down? What if we really could unlock the full potential of mankind, the potential God placed in us?"

"That's pretty exciting to imagine," I said. "I mean, that would be pretty big! I wonder how many Einstein's existed out there, but the world never knew them because they died as children in a genocide or lived somewhere with no access to education? If we could round up all those people and we could access all that potential, I suppose you're right ... it might take the universe to contain us," I pondered. "Maybe we do have the capacity to reach the stars or to cure diseases. Heck, maybe we really could even cure cancer or prevent heart attacks."

"Or strokes ... or dementia ... or Alzheimer's," Carl almost whispered, his voice cracking. "Wouldn't that be tragic, wouldn't it be absolutely tragic if that's what God had in mind the entire time and we failed to cooperate with His plan?" his voice quivering with emotion.

I could tell Carl was having a moment of grief about Mary, and this time I was smart enough not to say anything. I can only imagine how robbed he must have felt about the past 25 years, for his wife to still be alive, yet unable to join him during their golden years. I heard a couple loud sniffs before Carl cleared his throat. We sat in silence the remainder of the night prior to drifting off to sleep.

I have to admit, I've never seen the night sky the same way since that conversation with Carl. What if earth is not just our destination, but rather, our starting line? Is it possible that perhaps the reason God made the universe so big is because that's how big He made our potential? Is it that He knew if we were to ever get out of our own way and embrace what He always meant for us to be, that we would far outgrow this planet and would have to expand outward? Imagine what beauties and wonders exist out there in that amazing night sky still silently waiting for someone to finally see them? Imagine the empty worlds waiting to be inhabited, alone and unappreciated because we aren't there yet. What if God made it all for us, the whole universe and each of its wonders? How pathetic would it be if that were the case, and we are missing out on all of it because we continue to fight and kill each other over this tiny speck in which we currently dwell?

Yes, now, thanks to Carl, when I look into the night sky, I find it bittersweet as I fear I may not just be gazing into the limitless heavens; I fear I may also be looking at our unachieved potential. Perhaps, in that magnificent sky, we are not looking at something to show us how small we are, but how big we are meant to be and have refused to become.

Chapter 8
Drowning Topless

The next morning we got off to an early start and within a couple of hours had made our way down to the tribal village just upstream from the falls. After obtaining our camping permits, we hiked two more miles, passing Rock Falls, before rounding a corner, revealing the magnificent Havasupai Falls on our right. We stood for a moment taking in the dramatic scene of the large waterfall descending into its pool of blue-green waters before cascading downstream through a series of smaller pools. In light of our conversation the night before, I better understood what Carl meant and, in that moment, was quite thankful to be human, with the capacity to appreciate such stunning beauty.

After a few moments, we continued down the trail alongside the falls to the campground below. Being that it was just the two of us, setting up camp didn't take long. It was warm that day, and after several hours on the hot, dusty trail, we were ready for the refreshing waters that awaited us. Using the constant roar from the base of the falls as our guide, we headed back up to the main pool to catch a swim in the chilly waters.

This is where I learned Carl is not only interesting; he's a little crazy, too. The force of the water at the base of the falls is overwhelming, with small droplets stinging your face and body like tiny pieces of sand in a dust storm.

"Let's swim and find it!" Carl yelled over the deafening roar as he waded out into the waters and started swimming into the mist. "Find what?" I yelled, but he couldn't hear me. Not to be outdone by a guy in his 70s, I followed Carl, swimming to the right of the massive column of water. The current was powerful, tossing me all around and pushing us away from the base. I continued to watch as Carl disappeared behind the watery curtain.

Due to the sharp travertine rocks that make up the area, it is wise to swim with some sort of footwear so as not to cut up your feet, but the downside of that is it's more difficult to swim with shoes on. Fighting the strong current and sheer terror, I was able to make my way behind the falls where I saw Carl, who had now climbed up on a hidden ledge behind the waterfall. Clinging to the rocks, I scrambled out of the water and climbed up next to him. With us were a

Naked

handful of college kids who had made their way to the ledge from the opposite side.

"What are you looking for back here?" I yelled to Carl.

"What do you mean?" he hollered back against the deafening roar.

"You said let's swim and find it," I replied

Carl let out a laugh. "No! I said, 'Let's swim behind it!'" he clarified.

I chuckled, but was slightly disappointed that Carl hadn't stashed some sort of a secret treasure back here.

Although it was difficult to talk, I quickly surmised from the logo on their T-shirts that the college kids who were with us were some sort of church group. This was confirmed moments later as we all took turns jumping back into the water and letting the powerful current shoot us back out from behind the falls towards the edge of the pool. We climbed out of the pool and were standing at the edge with three young men and a young lady as their last two friends, both female, jumped off the rock one at a time and swam over to us. When the girl who went first came up for air, it was obvious there was something wrong based on the look on her face. She had an expression of panic as the current moved her toward us but her arms didn't seem to be working and she was having trouble keeping her head above water. As she got closer, it was apparent why: her arms were folded tightly over her chest, and trailing her in the water was a bright red bikini top. "Oh, my God!" she half yelled in a mortified tone before gulping and choking on a mouthful of water.

Not wanting to gawk, I found myself averting my eyes, noticing her male church friends did the same thing. I looked back when I heard a loud splash and noticed Carl dove in and was helping her get to shallower water so she could stand on her own while the second girl to jump in the water had retrieved her top and was on her way over. I was immediately embarrassed by the fact that with the exception of Carl, everyone else was so busy trying not to look at her that we failed to realize she actually needed help due to her reluctance to move her arms to swim. Thankfully, other than a little embarrassment, the girl was fine and her female companions helped her reassemble her wardrobe. Deciding we had experienced enough excitement for the evening, we headed back to our campsite.

There are no campfires allowed in the campgrounds, so at night the darkness of the canyon was dotted with propane lanterns at every campsite except ours, where the only light came from the dull red glow of our cigars. I was really glad when I learned Carl liked cigars as I don't smoke them often, but they have become a backpacking tradition for me. One of my favorite hiking rituals is to conclude my day by kicking back in my chair, after an evening bath in a cold creek. With my gross, sweaty hiking clothes drip-drying on a tree branch after being washed in the creek, I donned my cozy, dry camp clothes and a beanie to keep my bald head warm. There is nothing like a good cigar to usher in the night as dusk fades to darkness and the stars slowly come out one by one.

"Carl, you were a real hero today, the way you jumped in to help that maiden in distress," I needled.

Although it was too dark now to see his expression, I knew him well enough to know he was displaying a mischievous grin, an expression he would get now and then when thinking something of questionable appropriateness.

With a small chuckle, he replied, "Well, at my age, you don't know how many more chances you're going to get to find yourself in a position like that. You can't let those opportunities get past you."

"Hey, don't forget you're still a married man," I scolded sarcastically, mocking judgment in my voice.

"That I am," he laughed. "And I had to tell that young girl several times! Can you believe the way she shamelessly threw herself at me like that?" he laughed. "She clearly planned the whole thing."

"I'm sure it was your grandfatherly presence and flowing locks of silver hair that she just couldn't resist," I said.

"Clearly ... it drives women wild," Carl said in a teasingly egotistical voice, "and most men, too," he added.

With that we both broke out into laughter, unable to maintain the conversation due to the ridiculousness of it all.

"Isn't it funny, though?" Carl asked in a more serious tone. "All that girl had to do was swim, and she would have been fine; but instead, she chose to nearly drown rather than move her arms and uncover her chest."

"Ha, yeah, and her church buddies and I found it more important to look away than to actually help her," I commented sheepishly. "Until you jumped in, I didn't even realize she was in trouble."

"That's the thing," Carl continued, "she never really was in trouble; all she had to do was swim, but she created trouble because she was more concerned with covering her humanity than keeping her head above water."

"Hmm, in a way, that's the perfect analogy for sin," I thought out loud. "To open up and reveal it might be embarrassing, but at least it frees us to continue moving forward in life. When we spend all out time trying to hide it, it can drown us."

"Yes!" Carl said emphatically. He continued, "And really, what's more embarrassing? Being a perfectly healthy grown adult who knows how to swim but dies drowning, or having a couple of people see your tatas?" Carl paused. "We've got it so backwards. You're right: this is the perfect analogy for sin. For example, everybody on earth, male or female, has a rear end, yet we cover them up and get embarrassed if someone sees ours. They're like a nose or a belly button! Everyone has one!" he laughed. "How stupid is that?! And guess what? Just like everybody on earth has a butt, every one of us also has a struggle of some sort, something that enslaves us; and rather than just accepting that and being transparent about it, we all cover those things up and would rather drown inside than reveal our secrets."

"Well, I honestly can't provide a logical answer as to why we cover our rears; that does seem a little silly, but when it comes to our sins, I think it would be a lot easier if we didn't feel we'd be judged," I said flatly.

"True," he confirmed, "but would you rather be judged and live life, or keep your secrets and die inside? Transparency, man! That's what Jesus was all about! Be real! He flipped out on hypocrisy. He told us to become like children. He tells us to confess our sins. What is confessing our sins? It's being real! It's being transparent!" he said with his voice growing in passion. "He also told us not to judge one another. What does not judging do? It creates an environment in which it is easier to confess! This takes us back to being real again! Not judging makes it easier for people to be real!"

"Well, if everyone would do it, that would be one thing," I said, "but I'll be honest: in our current social environment, that sounds pretty terrifying."

"It is scary, I agree," Carl said, "but is fear what we are supposed to be about in the church? Because when I look at the church today, I don't see love; I just see fear. Fear of being judged, fear of being revealed, fear of going to hell, fear of not getting into heaven, fear of sinning... FEAR! FEAR! FEAR! Whatever happened to *LOVE?!*"

I sat silently pondering what he had said. I knew he was right, and I knew I was guilty of most of the things he had rattled off.

"We are so blind as to how opposite we are of what God had in mind," he said quietly. "You can see it even in the way we dress for church! For generations we would put on our 'Sunday best,'" he said. "Normally our Sunday best consisted of the best possible clothes we had, clothes that we never wore in daily life but were intended to make us look as good as we possibly could, hiding our normal tattered appearance. We call it 'modesty,'" he mocked. "We cover our bodies from our chin down, revealing as little as possible of the body God gave us, the body made in His image. Just like Adam and Eve, we are ashamed to show it. At least they stopped with the leaves. We've taken it way farther than that, covering up everything else. And the only thing we cloak even more than our bodies is our hearts!" Carl concluded emphatically.

After sitting pensively for a few moments, a thought occurred to me.

"Okay, I've got a question for you," I piped up.

"Shoot," Carl replied.

"So to play devil's advocate here, it just occurred to me that Jesus wore clothes. If He was all about this authenticity, shouldn't He have been walking around naked?" I asked.

"That's a fair question," Carl conceded. "I've actually wondered about that one, too, and I don't really have a good answer for it other than the fact that maybe the world just couldn't handle that kind of transparency."

"Yeah, maybe," I said, still unsure of a good answer.

"He was naked at the end, though," Carl added.

"I don't remember anything in the Bible about Him ever taking His clothes off," I said, confused.

"On the cross," Carl said grimly. "They would have stripped Him completely naked on the cross. It was part of the Roman's way of trying to cause the prisoners maximum humiliation prior to death. The entire ghastly scene, revealed for all to see, put on display up on a cross. Those guys spent hours up on those things, sometimes days even! The blood, the guts, the urine, and defecation. All of it, every messy, unsettlingly aspect of our humanity, everything we are used to covering up and hiding in the privacy of our lives, just put out there for the whole world to see."

"Wow," I said sadly. "We are so messed up that we actually use the very image of God, our own bodies and its natural functions, as methods of enhancing torture." I felt a lump growing in my throat as it dawned on me as to how insulting that is to God! This gift and honor God gave us by creating us in His image was not only covered up, but it was mocked and seen as a source of humiliation.

"Did you know there was a parallel between Christ on the cross and Adam?" Carl asked.

"Why, because they were both naked?" I guessed.

"Oh, it goes a lot farther than that." Carl proceeded, "I can't officially prove this first part, but it's what I believe in my heart and yes, it starts with the idea that they were both naked. Adam went from naked with no shame to covering himself due to shame."

"Okay, I'm with you so far," I said.

Carl continued, "I'd like to believe that Christ, on the other hand, would have seen shame in having to cover His body since it was the image of God. So He would have gone from being ashamed of being covered His whole life, to being stripped naked and having no shame."

"Hmm, that's a very interesting theory," I said. "And you're right, that's hard to prove; but if you are right, that would be really powerful! I'll have to think on that part a bit."

"The rest is pretty obvious," he said. "Do you remember Adam's curse?" he asked.

"Yeah, he was going to have to work by the sweat of his brow and the ground would produce thorns and stuff for him," I said, trying to remember it exactly.

"You think it's coincidence that Christ had a crown of thorns placed on His brow?" he asked.

"Wow, that is fascinating!"

"Also, don't forget that when God created Eve, He opened up Adam's side to pull out the rib," Carl paused. "We always think of Adam as being perfect and with no blemishes, but actually, he would have had a wounded side," Carl pointed out.

"And they pierced Christ's side," I said slowly, with the symbolism clicking for the first time. "Holy smokes ... you're blowing my mind right now!"

"There's still more," he laughed. "When Christ was taken off the cross and placed in the tomb, do you remember where the tomb was located?"

"Um, well, I seem to remember there being something about it being located in a garden," I replied. Upon saying the word *garden*, the connection to the Garden of Eden finally clicked, causing me to chuckle, a little putout at the fact I never saw all this.

"That's right, it was in a garden," Carl said, "as was also the case when He was arrested in the Garden of Gethsemane," he added. "So where Adam and Eve found death in a garden, Christ rose to life in a garden. Do you remember what was left in the tomb?" Carl asked.

"Huh ... yeah," I said with my mind racing. "His grave clothes ... after His resurrection, His coverings ... His clothes were left behind ... wow!" I whispered, mystified. "Where Adam put clothes on, the resurrected Christ left them behind!

"Do you remember who the first person was to find Him?" Carl inquired.

"Yeah, it was Mary, wasn't it?" I answered.

"That's right. Do you remember who she mistook Him for?"

"I do," I said, another parallel clicking. "She mistook Him for the gardener ... Adam was the gardener in Eden ... Amazing! So the whole scene re-creates and restores Adam," I realized.

"Not just Adam," Carl said. "When Mary found Him, they were the only ones there, so now you have a man and a woman in a garden, just like Eden. But this time, instead of the woman speaking the words that led to the man's death, the woman gets to speak the first words, proclaiming the resurrection of man back to life! Just like Christ was the restored Adam, Mary gets to be the restored Eve!"

"I don't even know what to say to all that!" I exclaimed. "I'm literally blown away by all this. I've never seen any of these connections before!"

"But wait!" I thought. "Again, shouldn't He have been naked again when she found Him? I'm a little confused by that."

"I think that's why He wouldn't let her touch Him," Carl speculated. "I'm not sure He was physically fully human anymore after the resurrection, so if that was the case, things might have changed a little bit. That's all I can think of."

"Hmm, well, either way, I think the symbolism of it all is still pretty strong," I said, taking one last puff on my cigar before snuffing it out in the sand. "As usual, you've given me a lot to think about," I said, gratefully.

"Ha, well, good," he said. "I'm getting tired and I probably better get to bed before that young siren from the waterfall comes looking for me again," he laughed. "As a married man, I do carry the irresistible burden of being forbidden fruit!"

I started laughing so hard I spit the water I was in the process of drinking halfway across the campsite before choking on the remnants, which in turn caused us both to laugh even harder.

"Good point!" I finally blurted after a few gasps of air and wiping tears from my eyes. "You'd better hide in your tent, quick!"

Chapter 9
True Love Never Ends Well

In all, we camped three nights, spending our days exploring some of the different side canyons and waterfalls, including the largest of them all, Mooney Falls. Meanwhile, our evenings were filled philosophizing and solving the problems of the world while enjoying cigars. After the long hike out, we had nearly a 7-hour car ride back home to look forward to.

"This might seem like a stupid question," I started, "and I'm not trying to be difficult or anything, but based on all of these theories and interpretations you have about covering up the image of God by covering our bodies, are you proposing people stop wearing clothes?"

Carl let out a hearty laugh, "Boy, that would be something, eh?" he said with a big smile. "To answer your question, in an ideal world, yes, but unfortunately, we don't live in an ideal world."

"I've been thinking a lot about what that would look like," I said.

"I bet you have," Carl retorted suspiciously.

"Ha, not like that," I answered. "But other than protection from the elements, there really isn't a logical reason for clothing. I wonder how much of our societal obsession with sex is directly related to the fact that we wear clothes. I wonder if that actually enhances the infatuation rather than dissuading it."

"Oh, I think it definitely has," Carl agreed. "Think about it: if you want to create intrigue and curiosity about something, you cover it up or hide it, make it taboo. If we lived in a world where nobody wore clothes, do you think pornography would exist? Or at least exist with nearly the popularity it does today?"

"Hmm, yeah, I guess you're right," I pondered. "I suppose the biggest draw to that, especially for younger guys, begins with the curiosity. Take away the curiosity and there's not much demand for it."

"Well, look at it this way," said Carl. "The audience for pornography pretty much consists mostly of males, and men are visual. On the other hand, the romance novel industry is mainly geared toward women, who are much less visual and much more emotionally driven. So we have two industries, each fantasy based, that can almost be cut right down gender lines as to their popularity, agreed?"

"Sure, I would agree with that," I confirmed.

"So look at what happened in the Garden! Men are visually stimulated and all of a sudden we start covering up, so men became deprived of the beauty of the female figure that we would have been able to visually appreciate all the time. And not only deprived, but now shrouded in mystery, generating a dysfunctional and warped obsession with it."

"Okay," I said, confirming I was still following.

"On the other hand, we not only hid our bodies, we also hid our hearts," Carl continued. "Before eating from the tree, women who are emotionally driven would have had full access to what men were thinking and feeling because we wouldn't have hidden that from them. So for the woman, when sin entered the picture, the male psyche that she would have had constant access to in all men would have been deprived from her, creating its own mystery and a dysfunctional and warped obsession on her side." Carl surmised.

"So you're saying the story of the Garden also explains our sexual dysfunctions?" I asked.

"Well, kind of," Carl reasoned. "It just seems to me that each aspect of what took place in the Garden, the covering of our bodies and the covering of our hearts, is what generally seems to motivate and affect both genders. Porn is primarily visual and mostly affects men, and romance novels and chick flicks are primarily emotional and mostly appeal to women. There are exceptions, of course, but in general, that seems to be the case."

"I think it's also important to point out that both of those industries deal with pretty much make-believe situations," I cautioned.

"They do," he said, "but they are make-believe situations that appeal to *real* desires. So whether the situations are real or not doesn't really matter. Dysfunctional and unlikely as they are, people flock to those industries not because the situations are real but because the feelings, desires, and wants that the fake situations address are the same feelings, desires, and wants that *actually* exist in real people."

"Interesting," I said, considering the idea.

"Now, I'm sure we'd find a way to replace it with some other dysfunctional behavior, but who knows?" Carl said. "But it goes beyond just sex," he continued. "Clothing segregates us in so many other ways. We use our clothing to convey status and wealth, stuff like that. I can put on designer jeans that cost $300, and really the sole purpose is just to broadcast to everyone else how much money I have."

"That's true, I guess; it does seem like the way people are dressed is one of the first judgments we make about them," I said. "In fact, according to my wife, every time I go out in public with a shirt that doesn't match, apparently every woman in the world notices and wonders what wife would let her husband dress like that," I laughed.

"That's quite a burden for you ... and her ... to carry," Carl laughed. "I used to joke with Mary that I dressed that way to repel them from me since I was so committed to her. But she would say I was repelling her, too!" Carl spaced for a second with a nostalgic sigh, "I sure miss bantering with her."

I looked over at him and noticed he appeared lost in a memory, staring out the window at the barren northern Arizona landscape.

"I'm probably out of place here, Carl," I started, "but situations like yours really make me wonder about God sometimes."

"How do you mean?" Carl asked.

"As a cop, I see all kinds of bad things that happen to people. Sometimes it's from their poor choices, but other times it's just random stuff that happens to people. Like Mary's stroke ... how can stuff like that be part of His plan?"

"Yeah, I struggled with our situation for quite a while," he replied. "Right after I had to put her in full-time care, I was feeling pretty sorry for myself. But then it occurred to me ... our relationship was destined to leave me with a broken heart — it was inevitable."

"Well ... that's a pretty pessimistic view on things," I chuckled. "I suppose you have some context for that statement?"

Carl laughed, "Yeah, it does seem pretty pessimistic," he smiled, "but it was right there in the beginning, some of the first words we uttered to each other on our wedding day were: '... till death do us part.' Eventually it hit me; if you live long enough, one way or another *every* meaningful relationship ends with a broken heart. That's the risk with love. Someday someone will cheat on you, or leave you, or betray you, or get sick ... or under the best possible circumstances ... they just die."

"Wow, you're really a bright spot today!" I said, trying to lighten the mood a bit.

"Ha, I'm sorry. I'm really not trying to be depressing," Carl said. "It's actually a very beautiful thing!"

"Really?" I asked. "This should be good."

"To love someone is to become so vulnerable to another person that you give them your heart with full knowledge it will one day be broken as a result and deciding it's worth it," Carl answered. "It's the ultimate sacrifice."

"Hmm …" I pondered. "Kinda makes you want to make sure you're the one who dies first," I said with mild sarcasm.

Carl smiled, "Yeah, I know what you mean, except that would be to wish the broken heart on your partner, which wouldn't be love. So in the case of Mary, I'd be lying if I said I don't get depressed sometimes. But when I do, I try to remind myself there was no way it was going to turn out well because true love can't end 'well.' It can only exist well. That helps me to actually be thankful for the way things are now, because I take comfort in the fact that I'm the one who gets to carry this burden, rather than her. I find relief that she's not the one having to care for me."

"So …" I concluded, "true love is loving someone so much that you're willing to allow your heart to be broken by however your relationship ends with them, and determining it to be worth it, and then hoping, in the end, that you *get* to be the one with the broken heart, so as to spare your loved one that pain."

"Yep," Carl confirmed. "When you get home, don't neglect time with that beautiful family of yours. There's no such thing as 'happily ever after,' Liam. If you wait for it, it will never come. There can just be 'happy right now.' Don't miss it while it's here."

We sat quietly in the car for a few minutes as the conversation hung in the air.

"Kinda makes you wonder if loving is worth it when you look at it from that perspective," I said.

"It really does," agreed Carl, "and for some people it's not. They choose to lock their hearts up and give them to nobody. They don't see people as relationships but as things to manipulate to get what they want. They care about nobody but themselves ... which is the greatest irony of all, because in the end, they still lose what they love most ... they lose themselves ... and their hearts die well before their bodies, leaving them able to exist ... but never really love."

"I guess that's really what made Jesus so different, isn't it?" I realized. "He knew we would all break His heart, and He just kept putting it out there. All the way to the very end, offering forgiveness even while they were killing Him."

"He was the perfect model of love," Carl agreed.

We again sat in silence for a few minutes. I truly enjoy talking about things like this, but sometimes the concepts are so heavy, I can only ponder them for a short time before needing some levity.

"I'll tell you this," I said, finally breaking the silence and returning to our original conversation, "if people didn't wear clothes, it would sure make my life easier as a cop!" I laughed, "Yep, pretty sure that guy doesn't have drugs, stolen property, or weapons on him ... and if he does ... well, he can keep them!"

"I'm sorry," Carl said, cracking up. "I just can't stop laughing at the mental image of a bunch of naked cops running around wearing only their duty belts!"

"If anything would discourage crime, I suppose it would be the idea of that coming after you," I laughed.

Chapter 10
Carl's Church

Whenever either Emma or I take a trip of any sort without the other, it's pretty much our marital policy that a date night will take place as soon as possible after the event. Normally the idea is for it to be just the two of us, but Emma surprised me on this one by suggesting we invite Carl to join us for dinner.

After a couple of emails, arrangements were made for a Friday night rendezvous at a little pub Carl suggested downtown.

When we arrived, we were seated prior to Carl showing up. The place was a small hole in the wall that only sat 20-30 people total. It was dimly lit with a jazz band consisting of mostly gray hairs, playing on a small stage in the corner near a pool table and a dart board that was barely distinguishable from the hundreds of signs hanging on the walls. It seemed like the kind of place that had regulars as it was somewhat obvious that our waitress, a gal who appeared to be in her mid-40s, with red hair, bright red lipstick, and a sleeve of tattoos on her left arm, seemed irritated to be dealing with newcomers. As we were nibbling on an appetizer, I heard the drummer suddenly yell out, "Hey, Carl!"

I looked up to see Carl with a big grin give a little salute and point to the band members who all waved in return.

"Well, aren't we the popular one!" I said as Carl slid into our booth, still smiling widely.

"I've been here a few times," he remarked.

Our waitress returned to the table and this time, much more politely, she re-greeted us in her Brooklyn accent, "You guys didn't say you were friends with Carl!" Then, turning to him, continued, "How have you been, hon? You getting your regular?"

"I am, thank you, Shirley. How's little Sarah doin'?" he asked.

"She's growin' up so fast, Carl, it's unbelievable. She starts junior high next year!"

"Are you serious?" Carl exclaimed. "Man, it sure goes by fast! Give her a kiss for me when you get home tonight!"

"I will, hon. We've missed you around here lately."

"Yeah, I've been doing a lot of traveling, but I'll be around a lot more now," Carl said.

As Shirley left to place our order, Carl turned to us, "This place is owned by a friend of mine named Phil," he explained. "He's a good dude, but it doesn't look like he's here tonight."

Shirley returned with a large frosty mug of cold beer for Carl. "Here you go, hon, your favorite. I'll be back with your guy's food in a bit."

"Thank you, sweetheart," Carl replied with a wink.

"So I'm guessing you've been here more than once?" I joked.

"Oh, yeah, this place is like my home away from home," he said.

With that, the guys in the band finished a song and announced they were taking a 5-minute break. To Carl's delight, each of them came over and introduced himself to us while giving Carl hearty hugs.

"Hey, Carl, you just barely ordered your food, why don't you spot me a song or two," said the bass player, a guy named Daryl, an African American with long, greying dreadlocks. At this, the rest of the band chimed in, "Yeah, come on, brother, jam with us a bit."

Carl flashed a sheepish grin, "I'd love to, guys, but I don't want to be rude to my friends here."

"Are you freaking kidding me?" Emma exclaimed. "No, you get up there, we want to hear this!"

Carl looked at me like a boy who had just been ordered to do something by his mother, "You better listen to her, buddy, you don't want to get on her bad side," I laughed.

Carl agreed, "Well, I guess I better do what I'm told, then!" he said cheerfully.

When Carl slid out of his seat and approached the stage, the rest of the bar gave out a small cheer. As soon as he left, Daryl took his place and grabbed some of our nachos, "I'm sure he won't mind if I steal a couple of these," he said with a grin.

Carl picked up the bass, took a seat on the stool, and after a "two, three, four!" count, they were off and playing. Not only was Carl good, really good, he was also a joy to watch play. With eyes closed and head bobbing all around, it was like the music flowed right through his body to his fingers that played effortlessly, his left hand hitting every fret perfectly while his right plucked away at the strings.

"This guy is not even real!" Emma shouted to me over the festive music. "Is there anything he doesn't do?"

I laughed, "He certainly is full of surprises!"

After two songs, our food arrived and to the applause of the entire pub, Carl came back to our booth and switched places with Daryl. With small beads of sweat now on his forehead, Carl was beaming with a large grin. "Ah ... that felt good," he said, like he had just received a massage. "I needed that!"

"You, sir, are something else!" I said, smiling in admiration.

"This place is my church," he quipped with a smile as he sipped his beer.

"How long have you been coming here?" Emma asked.

"Oh, I don't know, maybe five or six years now," Carl guessed. "I've always loved their music."

"You know, you told me once you were a minister, Carl, but did you ever pastor at an actual church?" I asked.

"No, I never did," he responded. "I went to seminary and did all the studies, but when it came down to it, I realized that places like this were where I wanted to meet people, to develop friendships. My last year in seminary, I was taking an advanced Greek class. This one particular day I walked in at the beginning of the semester right off a backpack trip; in fact, I barely made it to class in time and was unshaven and still in my sweaty hiking clothes. The professor looked right at me and said that from now on, I was to show up in class, dressed to present myself in a manner that was worthy of the gospel of Christ, and that if I couldn't do that, then not to bother continuing the class.

"Really! I'm sure that went over well," I scoffed.

"It made quite the impression on me," Carl said. "I was finishing up my Doctorate in Theology at that time. I stood back up from my desk; and as I walked out, I told him that it was unfortunate that Jesus would not have been able to attend this class since He dressed like He was homeless."

"Nice," said Emma, "good for you!"

Carl chuckled, "Well, it might have been a bit of a hothead thing to do. But after that, I re-evaluated what I really wanted to do, and I came to the conclusion that I wanted to reach people wherever they might be. I didn't want people looking at me like the minister guy and being made to feel like they needed to apologize to me every time they said a swear word, or get weirded out every time I showed up to a backyard party at a neighbor's house where people were drinking. At the same time, I didn't want to be restricted in what I could do, either. I wanted to be able to drink a beer with a guy who was having a hard time or smoke a cigar while discussing life with a friend, and not have the church looking over my shoulder telling me how I'm supposed to behave."

"I can't argue that you probably do have a lot more freedom than you otherwise might have had," I surmised.

"Yeah, and I also didn't want to be a 'preacher,' if you know what I mean. Don't get me wrong, I loved delivering sermons when I got the chance; but after a while, there's pressure to bring a great sermon every week," he said. "If you're not careful, you start to get nervous about keeping your job if your sermons start to suck, or if attendance goes down, or whatever. I mean, Jesus preached now and then, but it was only when He wanted to and was inspired to; it wasn't like He ever said, 'Oh, man, I really need to spend some time coming up with a sermon this week!' He mainly just focused on building relationships with people."

"You're really making me reconsider my position at the church," I said with a chuckle.

"Don't get me wrong. I do think there is a place for that," he said. "That's just not what I feel compelled to do.

Religions all over the world have people up on platforms telling their followers how to live. Christianity should be different than that because Christ was different than that. Let's face it, Jesus was all about love and relationship, and you can't have love and relationship from a pulpit or a stage or a television show. You can spread the information of Christ that way; but if you want to spread the love of Christ, you gotta get down into the messiness of people's lives and spend time there. It's relational, it's real, it's transparent, it's authentic, it's intimate," he said. "You can't waltz out on to a stage, deliver a message to 1,000 people and then expect to have a true relationship that way."

"So you're saying it should be more of a movement?" Emma asked, intently zeroed in on what Carl was saying.

"Yes, exactly," Carl confirmed. "It should be a person-by-person grassroots movement of love. We're in such a hurry all the time," Carl lamented. "We are so focused on reaching as many people as we can as fast as we can, and in turn, we end up with a very shallow Christian culture. People are trying, but all they have is what they've been told from pulpits. They don't have many one-on-one demonstrations of the relationships that true Christianity is built upon. We don't know what it looks like because we don't do authenticity. We just speak to the masses rather than mentoring the individual."

It suddenly clicked as to why Carl had so many friends all around the world; he treated each person he met like they were the center of his world when they were in his presence.

"Do you think I could hang out in a place like this and casually have a beer with these guys if I was the pastor of some large church?" he asked. "Either these people would have never accepted me because they would have suspected I was simply here to convert them, or my church would have fired me for being too worldly. I know all these guys, I know all their stories, and they all know mine! We love each other and care about each other. They all know where I stand.

"There's a guy named Dave, who is here sometimes. When Dave's here, I never order a beer because Dave's an alcoholic. How do I know that? Because I know Dave and he's shared that struggle with me. Daryl, up there on the bass, well, Daryl and I once sat right here in this booth and talked about a struggle he was going through in his marriage. We had known each other for several years prior to that and one of the things he told me was that he never felt comfortable around Christians, and how it blew him away that I was willing to have a beer with him. You see, I want to be free to adapt relationally to every situation and not be restricted by religion."

"It's like what the Apostle Paul said when he talked about becoming all things to all men or about eating meat sacrificed to idols," I observed, now realizing the deeper meaning. "If people offered him the meat, he ate it, knowing that the gods it was sacrificed to didn't exist; but if someone else there had a problem with it and freaked out, then he wouldn't eat it. That's interesting. He never crossed the line of doing anything wrong, but what He did was all relationship-based."

"That's right; there are no cookie-cutter relationships, Liam. Love demands we all custom tailor our relationships to each unique person we encounter. Our unique authentic selves to theirs, and as a result, no two relationships will ever look the same."

"I never really thought about it that way," I reflected. "But you're right, it does seem like there is a much higher priority to convert people to Christianity than there is to just love them whether they convert or not," I said grimly.

"That's why places like this are my church just as much as a revival tent," Carl said, "because for me, I've decided I want to be about relationship not religion; and relationship can happen anywhere and everywhere, but religion has its boundaries ... judgment being one of the biggest."

"So how were you able to come to so many different perspectives on church and religion?" Emma asked.

"Oh, I wasn't always this way," Carl admitted sheepishly. "I used to be as judgmental as anybody, but then a couple things happened that helped change that," he reminisced. "One was the way that professor made me feel in front of my class. That made a big impression on me as to how the church must make people feel sometimes. But another one was a weird dream I had once."

Carl continued eating, leaving Emma and me sitting in suspense.

"Okay," said Emma, finally breaking the silence with a laugh, "You can't just leave us hanging after saying something like that! What was the dream about?"

Carl smiled and took another bite and a swig of his beer before continuing. "I have to admit, I'm not always comfortable sharing it because it's often misunderstood when I tell it," he cautioned, "but here goes anyway. I'm not sure where it came from or what caused it, but I dreamt I died and was waiting to see God. I entered into a gigantic room, enormous, the walls were probably a mile high, and it was so vast, like being an ant standing in the middle of a gymnasium or something. Of course, it was decorated with gold and all the stuff you would expect to see in a heavenly room, and in the middle of it all was a giant throne where God was sitting. It was weird, though, He was so big, but it was like I couldn't really see Him that well, or at least all of Him anyway. At one point I looked around and the room was empty as far as I could see in every direction, and it suddenly occurred to me that, other than God, I was the only one there! After a few awkward minutes of silence, God finally spoke first, 'You're wondering where everyone is ...' He began.

"'Yes, I am,' I admitted.

"'They're all here,' God said gently.

"'I guess I just don't understand,' I conceded.

"'I made one soul,' God said. 'Every person that you have ever met, everyone you ever loved, ever hated, were ever kind to or mean to, every person that ever lived, saints, sinners, the powerful and the peasants, the wicked and the loving, winners and losers, every last one, with the exception of my Son, was you: you living life under their circumstances. Every time you judged someone or thought poorly of someone else, you were actually judging yourself living life under their exact conditions,'" Carl concluded.

"Wow, that's a pretty intense dream!" Emma exclaimed.

"It was," Carl agreed. "But Liam seems a little more skeptical," he smiled as he looked at me.

I should have known it was impossible to conceal my feelings from the ever-perceptive Carl, as even the slightest change of expression was enough to tip him off to one's thoughts. The pastor in me was kicking in, and in my mind I was searching for any scriptures that would give any credence to what he had just shared.

"I guess I just have a hard time buying the idea that we are all the same person living separate lives," I admitted.

"I don't think we are either," Carl agreed.

"But isn't that what you were just implying?" I asked.

"No," Carl clarified, "I said I went to bed one night and that was the dream I had. I don't think that's how things actually are, but it still forced me to completely change the way I looked at others. Now I look for a little bit of me in everyone else, no matter who they are, especially if I'm tempted to be critical of them."

I've never forgotten his dream; in fact it changed the way I looked at every "suspect" I ever dealt with from then on in my police career. Each time I had someone in the back of my patrol car that I had arrested, I tried to remember that perhaps I was meeting a version of myself under different circumstances. It really brought a new clarity to the "Golden Rule" Jesus talked about when He said to treat others as you would like to be treated yourself, or how we will be judged by the same measure we judge others. I'm thankful Carl felt comfortable enough to share that dream with us for as a result, I'll never see another person the same.

Chapter 11
Emma's Revelation

"That was really fun," Emma said as we drove home from the pub. "Does he always say things like that?"

"Pretty much," I replied. "It's like his mind operates on a different frequency than everyone else's."

"He definitely has some different perspectives, that's for sure," she added. "I still can't believe the way he just got up there and joined the band; that was amazing."

"Yeah, I didn't see that one coming," I admitted. "I had no idea he played any instruments. But now the long hair makes more sense," I said, causing us both to chuckle.

"You know, he really does have a point, though, with his reasoning for not becoming a pastor," I mused.

"Yeah?" Emma asked.

"Well, think about how often you hear about some pastor somewhere having a massive personal meltdown, you know, like an affair or a drug addiction or something. You think those guys ever felt like they could just come clean about their struggle?" I inquired.

"Unfortunately, I think there are a lot of churches out there that would fire any pastor that didn't appear perfect," Emma said. "I bet it's gotten better, but I can imagine that would have been especially true when Carl was younger."

"Yeah, so basically Carl has decided that he can just be a Christian, just love people and reach into their lives where they are, without having to carry the pressure of appearing perfect for a congregation somewhere. He can follow his instincts and do what he feels led to do in the moment," I surmised. "Like he said about having a beer with Daryl, if he was a pastor and did something like that in a public place, he'd be looking over his shoulder the whole time to see who might be there and see him. This way, he doesn't have to worry about it."

"I get that," Emma said, sounding almost like she was asking a question. "And maybe this isn't so much of an issue with Carl because he's so unique, but don't you think there is something to be said for having people to hold you accountable? Not like in a judgmental way, but in a way that helps keep people from slipping up?"

"Yeah, but I think that's why Carl talks so much about being authentic. Let's face it, for a lot of people, religion is like a teacher proctoring a test, the kids don't cheat because they know they are being watched, so their behavior is appropriate, but their hearts might not be. So they either don't cheat for the wrong reasons, or they hide their cheating really well so as not to be caught by the teacher. But the kids who authentically understand the material, don't need a proctor at all, they wouldn't cheat even if there weren't a teacher in the room because they know the material."

"That's a great analogy," Emma said, sounding impressed. "I think Carl is starting to rub off on you."

"Well, to be honest, I stole that from him," I sheepishly admitted.

Emma laughed, "That explains it! But you're right, uh, actually Carl's right. It seems like, the way I was raised anyway, religion spent more time telling me how to live rather than showing me why that was the best way to live."

"I liked it better when you thought I was right," I quipped. "I don't get to hear you say that very often." I continued, "One of the analogies Carl used as we were driving home from the Grand Canyon was the idea of a mother teaching her child to look both ways before crossing the street. Religion would be like the mother simply teaching the child to look both ways, but never explaining what to look for or why to do it. So out of obedience to his mom, the child will look both ways; but eventually, as he grows, the child might question his mother's teachings and decide to see what happens if he doesn't look both ways. If the child crosses the street without looking and nothing happens, then he might surmise that looking both ways is just some hocus-pocus ritual of his mother's. He will then continue to cross the street without looking, further reinforcing his mindset before eventually getting plowed over by a car."

"On the other hand, Christianity the way Christ taught it would be like the mother who teaches her child to look up and down the street for oncoming traffic so they don't get hit by a car. That kid will get it and will look both ways, not out of obedience, but out of understanding as to why that is best. To an outsider watching both kids cross the street, they both appear the same in that they both looked up and down the street, but in actuality each of them will be doing the same thing but for very different reasons."

Emma replied, "So basically, the kid that doesn't understand why he's looking both ways is the one who needs more accountability because he's more likely to violate the 'rule,' if you can even call it that?"

"Yeah, that's kinda how I understood it," I confirmed. "Both still need a little bit of accountability because we all make mistakes sometimes, but the one who authentically understands needs it less than the religious one who's just being obedient. I'm sure Carl would tell you that he's held accountable by his close relationships with people. He's transparent with them about his struggles early on so they don't have time to fester into secrets. For instance, he's been very open with me about the struggle it's been with Mary being sick. He fights being angry or feeling cheated, I mean, the guy's married but hasn't had sex in the last twenty-some-odd years. He told me it's gotten easier, but early on it was a challenge at times to remain faithful to her under those circumstances."

"Wow, that would be rough," Emma said. "That's some major discipline."

"He would disagree with that," I said. "He would say it takes major discipline if your reasoning for remaining faithful was because you're told you have to by your religion. But he truly loves her, and because he loves her, it's a different story. He still has desires and all, like sex for instance, but he doesn't just want sex. He wants to make love to *her*. He knows he can go out and have sex whenever he wanted to, but that's not what he wants. He wants her, and having intimate relations with someone else would leave him totally unfulfilled. In fact, not having sex with other people is actually more fulfilling to him because it's another act of love for her. So he would tell you he's authentically motivated by love rather than forcing himself to live in obedience to a system he's being constantly pulled away from."

I sat in silence waiting for Emma to respond and after a few moments, looked over to see her looking out the window, her eyes filled with tears. "That poor, sweet man," she lamented.

"It makes more sense now," she said a few moments later, wiping her eyes. "That's why Jesus was so forgiving of people's mistakes. He was way more concerned about love than obedience, because obedience was the result of love, not the other way around."

Her statement was so profound, "Obedience is the *result* of love, not the other way around." That thought would consume me for the rest of my life.

"Wow, now you're starting to sound like Carl," I laughed. "I can't have both my wife and my friends be smarter than me," I said with a smile.

"If that's the case, you'd better start finding dumber friends!" she laughed.

"I'll just make sure my next wife is dumb," I ribbed, bracing for a reaction.

"I'll just make sure my next husband is smart," she retorted with a sly grin.

Chapter 12
Till Death Do Us Part

Death notifications suck. Of all the calls we get as officers, these are some of the ones I dread the most. Few things in life are more awkward than knocking on the door of a complete stranger who is having a perfectly normal day, knowing I am about to destroy their world with the news I'm going to share. They don't even realize they are already having perhaps the worst day of their life.

To watch the kind smile melt away from their face as they lock eyes with you while you're standing there in uniform, and begin to realize that something is terribly wrong. You can almost see them begin to brace themselves for something awful as you open your mouth and the words seem to crawl out. Their reaction to what is being said seems delayed as they try to process such monumentally impactful information. Then it hits. The meltdown. That moment when all the air is sucked out of the room and absolutely nothing else matters as the most pure, raw, and human of emotions come pouring out. That moment when it doesn't matter who is around, it doesn't matter what we look like, who we are, or where we are from, nothing really matters. For those outsiders, not directly emotionally invested in the situation, the extreme awkwardness of standing there watching someone completely break down is difficult to describe.

The immediate temptation is to try to quell the situation. To begin to console and tell them it will be okay. All the while knowing it won't be "okay." It will be "okay" that you lost your daughter; it will be "okay" that your husband will never come home again; it will be "okay"? Really? It will be "okay"? No, it won't. You may eventually move on, you may come to terms with something like this, but it will never be "okay." I've learned that the temptation to say such things comes much more from my discomfort in the situation rather than theirs. Fortunately, I've never given into that temptation at work. No, rather than tell someone it will be okay, I've normally just stood there like an android, maintaining my official presence while in the midst of a flood of true human emotion.

What makes things worse is we often don't have a lot of information to share with these people who, after the initial tidal wave of shock subsides, naturally have a number of questions as to the circumstances surrounding the demise of their loved one. Many times things happen out of state, and we are sent on behalf of another law enforcement agency to track down next of kin, only knowing the name of the deceased.

This call wasn't quite as bad ... yet. I was asked by dispatch to contact a local hospice facility as one of their patients had died and they needed us to locate family members. I remember thinking that by speaking directly to the facility I'd at least be able to gather a little more than the absolute basics to share with this poor family when I contacted them. I also remember feeling a bit of relief that since this was a hospice case, the news shouldn't be quite as much of a shock to the family. I responded to the facility, which was in my beat, and spoke with the charge nurse at the front desk.

"Ah, you guys here for the lady who died?" she asked me and my partner, Brian.

"Yep, whatcha got?" I asked, pulling out my pen and notepad.

"Well, this one should be pretty easy, looks like it was a major stroke and she had a DNR," she said. "We need you guys to go contact her husband who lives nearby. We would have just called him, but he doesn't own a cell phone. It's really sad cuz he was just here about an hour ago."

Normally I would have had some wisecrack response for her about the guy not having a cell phone, but not this time.

My heart sank to the pit of my stomach as I immediately knew who I was on my way to contact.

"Officer? Officer? Are you alright?" the nurse asked.

"Hey, Liam, you okay, buddy?" my partner, Brian, asked.

I snapped out of my little trance to see both the nurse and Brian, looking at me strangely.

"Mary," I said softly.

"Excuse me? I'm not understanding you," the nurse answered, looking concerned.

"Mary Bennett? Is that your patient?" I asked, recomposing.

"Oh! Um, yes. I'm sorry, I didn't think we told your dispatchers," she said.

"Uh, how'd you know that?" Brian asked, bewildered, as dispatch had not given us that information.

"I know her husband," I said dryly. "There can't be too many guys out there who don't have cell phones."

At this moment I felt a number of emotions: sadness, a little bit of dread in having to go contact Carl, but most of all, shame. I felt shame in that all the time I had known Carl I had never come with him to visit Mary. I didn't even know in which facility she was living. How could I have never thought to meet the most important person in the life of one of my dearest friends?

We drove to Carl's apartment complex, and as we each exited our patrol cars, I was briefly overcome by a sudden anxiety. I had never seen Carl in a situation like this. After all, he had just seen his wife an hour ago and she was fine, now he's about to learn she's gone. My logical side told me Carl would keep his composure in any situation, but in this job I've learned that you can never really predict people's reactions to things.

We approached the door and knocked loudly. After a moment, I could hear footsteps approaching the door and with each one my stomach tightened with dread.

Carl opened the door, and upon seeing us, flashed a cautious grin, "Well, this can't be good, normally you'd just walk right in."

"Yeah, well ... unfortunately, we are actually here on an official call," I said.

"We got a crazed lunatic running through the complex or something?" Carl asked with a smile.

"Actually, I wish that was the case," I replied. "No, Carl, actually we are here because of Mary."

Carl's smile immediately began to melt away, and I saw *that* expression ... the same one I had seen so many times before. I can't really describe what it looks like, but it's the same every time: a mixture of denial, confusion, and the dread of someone emotionally bracing himself for something terrible.

I continued, "The care facility had us come find you since you don't have a phone ... shortly after you left this morning, Mary appeared to have had a massive stroke and passed away."

Carl's expression turned empty, his normal soul-piercing eyes now appeared hollow; rather than peering into me, I was now the one looking directly into his heart ... and it was breaking.

With tears welling up, he choked out the words, "I was just there ... I can't believe I missed her passing, I was just there."

With a couple of loud sniffs Carl wiped his eyes and retreated slowly a couple of steps to a chair near the door.

"This was my greatest fear," he continued. "I was always afraid I wouldn't be there when she died, that I'd be on one of my trips or something. I guess in the back of my mind, I always just kind of assumed it would be slow, that there would be a heads-up or something ... I ... I can't believe this ... I was just there ... I had nowhere to go ... I wanted to be there, to hold her hand and caress her hair and tell her it was okay, to escort her to the other side ... and I missed it ..." he said dejectedly.

"Would you like a ride back over there?" I asked, putting my hand on his shoulder.

"Yes ... yes, thank you, Liam," Carl said, standing back up.

I cleared my equipment from the front seat of my patrol car as Carl climbed into the passenger seat. Brian followed us in his car and we drove back over to the facility. As we entered, the entire staff, along with any patients who were ambulatory, were waiting for us. I followed Carl down the hall, now lined with caregivers silently watching, to finally see a woman I had heard so much about but never actually met.

As we turned the corner to enter the room, I had never seen so many pictures in my life: every inch on every wall was covered with them, hundreds of children consisting of every race, background, and nationality from all over the world.

Carl's eyes immediately locked onto a frail frame lying in the lone bed occupying the small room, covered from the chest down with the bedsheet, her arms and hands resting above the covers. He slowly approached and sat down into a chair next to her. He took her hand and with tears in his eyes quietly spoke.

"Well, Honey ... I'm so sorry ... I'm sorry I wasn't here for you ... but we did it ... we made it, sweetheart ... 'til death do us part ... we've honored our promises to love each other to the very end."

As I was watching this unfold, I was overcome by the tenderness of this moment; it felt almost sacred, and the presence of two police officers in the room seemed inappropriate. I looked at Brian, who was clearly thinking the same thing, and without a word we moved out into the hallway so Carl could have Mary all to himself for a bit.

When we exited the room, we were met by the entire staff, all of whom were wiping tears from their eyes. I had done enough of these types of calls to know this was very unusual.

"We love them so much," one of the nurses said, dabbing her eyes. "We've always considered them the example of what a perfect relationship looks like."

The hallway remained quiet, maintaining a reverent silence while Carl sat with Mary. Occasionally we could hear the unintelligible sound of his voice as he spoke to her, even an occasional chuckle. After almost an hour, Carl came out of the room. His eyes that had been hollow now had a little life back to them, his expression one of total peace.

"I want to thank all of you for the family you've become to Mary and me," he said to the staff. He then proceeded to individually address each person, giving every one of them a hug and expressing his gratitude. I could tell, though, that they all felt equally grateful to him. He had shown them what true love looked like; and in doing so, they also benefited from his travels for Mary as they were able to experience the world through him as well.

We completed our basic investigation and remained with Carl and the staff until the medical examiner's officer arrived to transport Mary's body, the standard procedure for anyone who dies unexpectedly.

My shift was ending so I went back to the station and changed out of my uniform before returning in my personal car to give Carl a ride back to his apartment.

"You gonna be okay tonight, buddy?" I asked as we walked up to his door.

"Yeah, I'll be fine ... actually ... I'm kinda looking forward to being alone for a bit to process all this," he said. "It hasn't set in yet, but my whole world just changed. Everything I've done for the last 25 years has been built around Mary. It's going to be strange with that not being the case anymore."

Carl arranged for a small memorial for Mary about a week later at the care facility, as that had become the closest thing they had to extended family. Although, "memorial" probably isn't the right word, "celebration" better encapsulates the mood of the event.

"It was always our dream to travel the world together," Carl said to the small crowded room, "but as you all know, fate had other things in store for us. So I've spent the last 20 years bringing the world here to Mary, and in turn, all of you. I've had the past week or so to try to figure out what I want to do next, and I've come to a conclusion. Mary never got to travel the world, so I've decided to take Mary to all of the places in her favorite pictures and spread some of her ashes in all those locations. So that means I'm going to be gone for a while, but don't worry. I will come back and I will continue to visit this place, because each of you have been the closest thing Mary and I have to family. I know how much my travels have meant to all of the others here, so I will continue to do so."

Naked

And just like that, three days later, Carl was gone. It would be a full year before I'd see him again.

Chapter 13
A Surprise Visit

Every time there is a knock at the front door, our house erupts into chaos. Our little yapper dog begins barking wildly, causing anyone near him to start yelling at him to be quiet. This yelling, of course, only serves to further excite him, causing even more barking. From within this ear piercing cacophony, someone will inevitably point out what is now obvious to everyone in the house. This time it was Emma.

"Someone's at the door!" she yelled from the top of the staircase, her arms full with a clean load of laundry.

"Really?" I replied sarcastically, as I began the journey from my seat in the living room to the front door. For most, this is simply answering the door, but for me it is also a quest to restore tranquility as I plead with whoever happens to be yelling at the dog to please stop, while at the same time trying to hush the annoying little animal. I don't like our dog ... but the kids love him, so he stays. He's about nine pounds of fluff and sound that would serve zero purpose in the wild other than to provide a snack for a hungry predator. We live near the desert, and once a fox made off with our cat. I liked the cat ... why couldn't he have taken the dog?

I peered through the blinds and chuckled as I recognized a face I hadn't seen in a little over a year. I flung open the door, "Carl!" I exclaimed, triggering the dog to go berserk again ... I hate the dog.

"How are you doing, friend!" Carl answered, setting his large backpack down and giving me a hug. "Sorry to drop in unannounced, but I was wondering if I could crash on your couch a couple of nights before I fly out again?"

"I don't think you're really sorry," I laughed, "but yes! We'd love for you to stay a couple nights!"

After Mary passed away, Carl got rid of what few belongings he had and moved out of his apartment, pretty much living out of a backpack, traveling the world. Normally someone dropping in unannounced like this would have driven Emma crazy, but Carl was different. Anytime he showed up, there was a great excitement to stay up late and listen to the stories of his latest travels while looking through pictures. One of the few modern purchases he had made was a small laptop computer to more easily preserve his adventures.

We promptly moved our daughter into her little brother's room to provide Carl an actual bed, rather than the couch. After a shower, a nap, and dinner, we gathered in the living room for a couple of hours while Carl caught us all up on his last year of travels before we sent the kids to bed.

"I've got a gift for you," Carl said with a grin as he began digging through his pack. "Let's see ... ah, there they are," he said as he pulled out two cigars. "I got these in Nicaragua."

Late fall in the Sonoran Desert produces some of the most beautiful evenings, gone are the scorching summer temperatures, and while the days can still be warm, the evenings are perfect for being outside.

"So where are you headed on your next trip?" I asked Carl while exhaling a plume of cigar smoke as we sat with our feet up on the patio table in the backyard.

"I'm not sure exactly," Carl replied, leaning back in his chair and pondering. "I'm thinking about putting all of my theories about embracing God's image to the test and going to a nudist resort."

"You're going to a nudist resort?!" I exclaimed, laughing loudly, "Have you lost your mind?!"

"I'm seventy-five, what do I care?" Carl retorted with a slight grin, holding his cigar in his teeth. "And I didn't say that I was going; I said I was thinking about going," he clarified.

"You're really taking this authenticity thing to a whole new level!" I said, wiping my eyes. I was laughing so hard they had started tearing up.

"My only concern is that the mentality at a resort might not encapsulate the innocence of authenticity in the way I'm seeking it," he snickered. "I'm afraid it might be centered more on exhibitionism than authenticity."

Still laughing, I replied, "Well, I guess there's only one way to find out!"

"True," he conceded, "but a resort is actually too upscale for me. But along those same lines, I learned there are some Pacific islands down near New Zealand where a number of the natives still live the way they have for hundreds of years. It's tropical so everyone pretty much runs around in their birthday suits and apparently they are quite welcoming of tourists."

"Yeah, I'll bet they are welcoming ... They'd probably love to have you for dinner," I quipped.

Carl laughed, "Well ... I suppose there are worse ways to go. As long as they fatten me up first before marinating me in beer and barbecue sauce. Either way, it's a place that's pretty high on my list to get to."

"I've got to admit, the image of a longhaired seventy-something running around naked among a bunch of islanders is rather amusing," I said. "I'll be sure to start tuning into National Geographic to watch for you!"

While we visited that night, I had an eerie sense that this might be the last time I would see Carl. I savored every moment of our conversation, wishing it would never end.

As expected, he actually followed through on his plans and spent the next year or two bouncing around a number of Pacific islands, which was proven by some very revealing photos he sent via email of him living in the jungle with the natives. I wasn't sure if I was more impressed with the fact that they actually took him in or that he was able to find an internet connection to send the emails. Our correspondence was random, often months went by between contacts as he would catch up when he found internet accessibility while transitioning from one place to another.

My feeling was almost right. That night was indeed the last night I would sit and visit with Carl, but it wasn't my final experience with him.

Chapter 14
Wandering Souls Never Die

One of the things I've learned as a result of my friendship with Carl is that wandering souls like his never die, mainly because nobody ever hears about it when they do. I haven't received any new messages from him in over ten years now, and although I remain hopeful that I'll get a surprise knock on the door, or a message out of the blue, I recognize it's not likely.

I think about him quite often; his impact on my life is undeniable, as I know it was for so many others. I suppose it's possible he's still out there somewhere, a thought that I find amusing as it allows my imagination to run with the possibility that he's sitting on a mountain somewhere as a great sage or the chief of some primitive island tribe. But most likely he died how he lived, not surrounded by crowds but in the presence of a few intimate friends with whom he had developed a deep and beautiful relationship.

One of Carl's greatest attributes was not just his unique perspectives on God, life, and the Bible, but also his ability to teach others how to look at things differently. Although I would never see him again, he continued to be an important influence on the rest of my life.

Prior to Carl, I used to see Christianity as a path to get from earth to heaven, a way to escape this troubled realm and find solace in a celestial paradise. But now, I see that Christianity is actually quite the opposite. When I see things like Jesus uttering the Lord's Prayer, saying, "... thy will be done on *earth* as it is in heaven ..." I have come to realize that Carl viewed Christianity as heaven's path back to earth, that our calling is not so much for us to get to heaven as it is for us to bring heaven here, that the story of the Bible isn't just one of atonement and forgiveness, but also one of restoration: a return to Eden, where mankind reclaims our place in God's hierarchy as the unashamed bearers of His image.

Jesus gave His life in this pursuit. All He had to do to escape His fate was the same thing Adam and Eve did, the same thing we've all done. Simply deny who He was, reject who God had created Him to be, and take His place among the hollow souls of this earth, each seeking to be something other than who and what we were truly made to be. Instead, He chose to stand out, not by seeking to be stand-outish, but by being exactly who He was supposed to be. He was so real, so authentic, so true to who God made Him to be that

Acknowledgements

He couldn't help but stand out as the only one at the masquerade not wearing a mask.

Even in our pursuit of being "Christ-like," we've missed the point. Jesus was the perfect Jesus, the Jesus God had in mind. When we seek to be "like Jesus," we are still seeking to be like someone else, for we are not Jesus. I learned from Carl that if we are to be "like Christ," we must be like Him in the way He was perfectly true to Himself. Carl would say to be "Christ-like" isn't to be like Jesus but to be like Carl, the perfect version of Carl, the Carl God had in mind when He first created Carl. For me it would be to become the perfect version of Liam, the Liam God had in mind when He uniquely created me. The Liam that would love God and love his neighbor: the real, authentic, naked, unashamed Liam.

The same would go for each and every one of us. God had a blueprint for each and every one of us, a blueprint that He created unique to each of us, one from which we have all strayed. Perhaps part of Christ's invitation is also a call to rediscover that person, the person God had in mind when He made you, a person we don't have to be ashamed of, physically, mentally, or emotionally.

Thanks to Carl, I no longer see Christ as an intimidating presence, someone who came to show us all that we are not; rather, I now see Him as the perfect model of everything we were meant to be, and still can be through the guidance and power of God.

I see Him as my guide on the path leading back to Eden, a place where I can finally discover and embrace the real me, and learn to see the real person God intended behind the masks we all wear. A place where we can end the charade and finally be authentic, finally be true, and finally shed the shame that comes with being naked...

Acknowledgements

Special thanks to:

- My wife, Karra — Thank you first and foremost for saying "yes" back in 1997 and changing my life forever! Through thick and thin you have been there with me and today I can't imagine life any other way than with you by my side. I love you forever.

- Glen Aubrey and the Creative Team Publishing Team — Five years ago, I contacted Glen with some writing I had done, and thanks to his prodding and encouragement I have now authored three books, quite a feat for a guy that hardly even reads a book, let alone writes one. Thanks so much for your help in making these dreams a reality!

Acknowledgements

- Melissa Quillard, Don Manack, and Tom Cleary— Thank you all for your willingness to take time out of your busy lives to proofread and provide feedback. Having an outside view point was invaluable to writing this, and your help was deeply appreciated!

- Rick Hicks—I know it was asking a lot of you to take time out of your busy life to read a manuscript and provide an endorsement for a complete stranger. I can't express how grateful I am for your willingness to take a chance on this project.

- Doug Momary—Like Rick, you also took a chance on a stranger, to place your name and reputation on this project. It doesn't escape me as to how generous of an act that is. Thank you so much for your time and kind words!

- Mike Atkinson—First off, thank you so much for coming up with Mikey's Funnies and bringing a positive spark every day into the lives of thousands who live in a world that seems to be so focused on the negative. I've completely enjoyed the friendship that has resulted from all of this and I'm so grateful for your endorsement. Thanks, friend! I still owe you coffee!

Acknowledgements

- Reverend Vernon Lintvedt—Thank you so much for taking the time to read through this manuscript. You didn't have to do this and your endorsement means so much. Thank you!

- Dennis Harrison—Thank you so much for your friendship and insights. It might seem like just a few lunches to you, but for me they have been mentoring experiences in leadership. Thank you!

- To every person who has ever shared a discussion of these concepts with me—There might be hundreds of you! You all know who you are; you are my friends. This book is the culmination of numerous conversations with countless people. Some of you I've known for years and others I've only met once, perhaps a passing conversation in a check-out line. Whatever the circumstance, contributions from all of you are represented here. Thank you all!

The Author

Will Hathaway is a man who has worn many hats. Born the third of four children to a hardworking cattle rancher and his wife near the foothills of the Patagonia Mountains in southern Arizona, he quickly learned what it meant to work with the tools God gave you, your hands. He spent most of his childhood and young adult years driving fence posts and breaking horses.

It wasn't until Will left home to attend Grand Canyon University in Phoenix that he realized how unique his upbringing truly had been. While pursuing a degree in Marketing/Business, he met and then married the love of his life, Karra. It was through Karra that he obtained his first job in ministry, cleaning toilets at his church and serving as Youth Pastor to junior and senior high school students.

In 1999, Will felt led to pursue his lifelong passion of full-time ministry and headed off to attend Grace Theological

Seminary in Warsaw, Indiana. Although he enjoyed his schooling, he took advantage of an offer to take a full-time position as a family life minister for a large church in Blytheville, Arkansas. Will and Karra remained in Arkansas for a year when they were surprised by the news of the upcoming birth of their first child.

They moved back to Arizona to be near family for the new baby. Will took a job in the investing/insurance market, but this vocation left him feeling empty and unfulfilled. During this time he continued his ministry pursuits as a volunteer youth pastor for their local church. The horrible events of 9/11/2001 became deciding factors that ended his short career as an investor.

Soon after, news started to spread that several local fire and police departments were hiring, so on a whim, he took a chance and was hired on as a police officer at a local department. Since his introduction to the police department in 2002, Will has served in many capacities including SWAT Negotiations.

Through the changes in his life, two things have remained consistent: 1) his call to ministry, with more than fourteen years in ministry beginning as a junior high and high school youth pastor and eventually as a college and career pastor; 2) his passion for his career in law enforcement.

Will is a family man with a strong sense of loyalty, especially when it comes to his wife, Karra, and their three children. He is an avid outdoorsman who enjoys spending time backpacking and camping in the New Mexico Wilderness. He can often be seen breaking horses on his parents' ranch, which still runs cattle today.

Will's diverse and multifaceted backgrounds provide him with unique perspectives on the world and God's interaction with it. Always seeking to gain a better understanding of his Creator, he is willing to ask the tough questions, many of which inspire his books.

Speaking Engagements and Products

Schedule Will Hathaway to speak at your event. Will Hathaway speaks for church services, conferences, Christian camps, and retreats.

Contact Will Hathaway at
www.Will-Hathaway.com

Products:

- ***What If God Is Like This?—Meet the God You've Never Known*** is the first book in Will's series entitled, *Released From Religion*. It asks the tough questions many have wanted to ask as they contemplate who God really is.

- ***The Human Side of Christ—Meet the Guy behind the God*** is the second book of the series. This book peels back the divine cloak of mystery surrounding Christ and His existence as God in the flesh, and focuses on the human personality that walked the earth. It asks, "Who was this man?" "What was He like?" "How can we relate to Him?" Momentarily view Christ as a man rather than as God and relate to Him human-to-human in very special and basic ways. Discover that studying His humanity actually enhances the perspective of His divinity.

- ***Naked*** Since the beginning, the story of Eden has captivated mankind in our pursuit of understanding not only God, but ourselves. But what if one of life's greatest secrets has been hiding for centuries in plain sight? What if the story of Christ was always meant to be viewed through the lens of Eden? And what if religion has accidentally overlooked one of the most important threads of truth contained in the Bible? A thread of truth that when exposed, will bring deeper clarity to our relationship with God, deeper intimacy to our relationships with others, and a deeper understanding of ourselves.

Watch as the life of a rookie beat cop is changed forever when he meets an elderly sage on a routine call. Using wisdom, perspective, and humor, *Naked* is a journey destined to transform the reader's understanding of God, life, and love.

CPSIA information can be obtained
at www.ICGtesting.com
Printed in the USA
FSOW01n0649130916
24911FS